How to Survive Your Child's Rebellious Teens

Also by Myron Brenton

The Privacy Invaders
The American Male
Sex and Your Heart
What's Happened to Teacher?
Sex Talk
Friendship
The Runaways

How to Survive Your Child's Rebellious Teens

New Solutions for Troubled Parents

MYRON BRENTON

J. B. LIPPINCOTT COMPANY
Philadelphia and New York

The quotation by Anna Freud in Chapter 2 is from *The psy-choanalytic Study of the Child*(New York: International University Press, 1958).

U.S. Library of Congress Cataloging in Publication Data

Brenton, Myron.
   How to survive your child's rebellious teens.

   1. Adolescence. 2. Adolescent psychology.
3. Parent and child. 4. Parenting—Case studies.
I. Title.
HQ796.B68825   301.43'15   78-26729
ISBN–0–397–01340–X

To Anna Waller-Zemon—
for all the worlds we've shared

Contents

Foreword

In 1977 the Carnegie Council on Children published a book based on extensive research into the way children grow up in America. Among other things, *All Our Children* by Kenneth Keniston, subtitled *The American Family Under Pressure*, dispelled the myth of family self-sufficiency; parents are not, nor were they ever, solely responsible for their children's successes or failures. The young are influenced and shaped by many broad social and economic forces—forces over which their parents have no control.

This revelation is at the heart of Myron Brenton's helpful book. He has written it for all concerned parents whose adolescent children's behavior ranges from relatively mild early rebelliousness to prolonged patterns of seriously distressing conduct through the teens and beyond. In its extreme forms, such behavior can be destructive not only to the adolescents themselves but to parents and siblings, disrupting the entire fabric of the family. But whether the problems are passing or prolonged, most parents are filled with guilt. "Where did we go wrong?" they wonder. Many are reluctant to admit their difficulties outside the intimacy of the family, or even to admit to themselves that the problems exist. Others in desperation seek professional help. Yet with perhaps a quarter million children —many of them emotionally disturbed, delinquent, or mentally ill—living in various private and public institutions, and countless other such children not institutionalized, clearly mental health professionals alone cannot fill the needs that exist in families in this country.

One of the most significant developments of recent years

is the self-help movement—including the mushrooming of mutual-support lay organizations. Many of us in the professional human service field are beginning to recognize these groups as offering the treatment of choice for a large number of individuals and families in distress of one kind or another. Such an organization exists for embattled parents: Families Anonymous, whose members mutually benefit from the support and shared experiences of others who are going through situations similar to, or worse than, their own.

Myron Brenton has made a thorough study of Families Anonymous, supplementing his considerable research in the professional mental health community. In *How to Survive Your Child's Rebellious Teens* he puts forward a self-help program for parents which can be meaningful, helpful, and reassuring. He demonstrates vividly that parents' problems with their adolescent children are not isolated agonies in "my family" alone but are prevalent among families everywhere. Through his marvelously selected and documented case histories of parents and children in turmoil, he identifies the apparent problems, the real problems, and the dynamics of the difficulties. He suggests methods by which parents can confront those difficulties unhampered by guilt or a sense of personal failure. And with insight and empathy he offers specific proposals as solutions for parents living and growing with their children. His primary purpose is not to instruct parents on how they can help or change their children. It is to point out ways in which parents can help themselves. But regardless of the author's intentions, his book is sure to serve as a preventive for problems not yet developed in families and as an important indirect help to the children for whose parents it was written.

> Earl J. Beatt
> Executive Director
> Family and Children's Service
> Minneapolis, Minnesota

Acknowledgments

Many, many people helped me as I researched and wrote this book. The vast majority are members of Families Anonymous, a self-help group for parents of highly rebellious adolescents. This group's goals and work I describe in the body of the book. Having gained varying but definite measures of relief from their years of worry and agonizing over their children and over their own predicaments, these mothers and fathers in various cities around the country freely shared with me their thoughts, feelings, experiences, and the know-how they had at last, however painfully, achieved with the help of the group. In order to preserve their anonymity (they were, in any case, introduced to me only on a first-name basis) I've changed their names and, where applicable, localities. I do want them all to know, though, how much of a contribution they made and how grateful I am.

I'd like to give special thanks to Marilyn and Ida Mae, both active in FA matters, both extremely helpful in acquainting me with FA principles and in facilitating my contact with other FA members.

And there are others to whom I owe a debt of thanks: the various mental health professionals whose advice I offer in the book; to Peg Cameron, my editor, for her sensitive editing of the manuscript; and to therapists Anna Waller-Zemon and Ellen Mendel for their careful professional reading of the book and for their sound, helpful suggestions.

M.B.

TAKING STOCK

1. You're Not Alone

THE TROUBLED YEARS

"Tears, turmoil, and trouble" is how one parent, the mother of a fifteen-year-old daughter, recently summed up life with an adolescent. Many other parents would fervently agree. Adolescence often is hard on the adolescents. Adolescence often is hard on parents, too—it can, in fact, be the most maddening, frustrating, sometimes harrowing time of their lives as mothers and fathers.

There's some comfort in the fact that this is nothing new. Since Grecian times bewildered, affronted adults have been writing about the excesses of adolescence. "I see no hope for our people if they are dependent on the frivolous youth of today, for certainly all youths are reckless beyond words," wrote the eighth-century poet Hesiod. "When I was a boy we were taught to be discreet and respectful of elders, but the present youth are exceedingly wise and impatient of restraint."

Each generation probably thinks its youth is the worst—and each survives; we can take comfort in that fact, too. It's hard to adopt the long view, however, when you're in the midst of a painful set of circumstances involving your own child. Here now is a father despairing about his oldest son, a seventeen-year-old boy—a boy who'd been a model youth, an honor student, suddenly truant from school in this pleasant Milwaukee suburb, suddenly staying out nights without telling his parents, suddenly arrested for shoplifting. Here's a mother distraught about her middle daughter—a girl who had always been sweet and docile but now, at twelve, is rude and hostile, hanging out with unkempt kids who never seem to sleep and who hate their mothers and fathers. She's also, her parents suspect, experimenting with marijuana. And here's yet another set of red-eyed parents; they sit nervously on a frayed couch at Daytop Village, a drug rehabilitation center in New York City, because their only child, a son of fifteen, has been popping uppers and downers; their world, once secure, has become a nightmare. For parents such as these, taking a long, benign view of adolescent rebellion and its excesses is next to impossible; they're in a crisis situation now, they want help now.

Of course, what constitutes a crisis to you may be relative to your experience and your threshold of tolerance. If, say, your early teenager is hostile and insulting to you these days, driving you wild, there are other parents out there, parents of heroin addicts, for example, who'd love to trade places with you. In fact, adolescent rebellion can range from the "normal" to the extreme—that is, from the child who plays hooky a few times, steals a handful of candy bars from supermarket shelves, talks back to his parents, and engages in a bit of vandalism to the child who's physically or psychologically addicted to drugs, stages a number of runaway episodes, refuses to attend school, and otherwise engages in self-destructive behavior that lasts for many months, possibly years, and keeps on escalating.

This book is intended to help anxious, worried, perplexed, enraged, or utterly despairing parents whose teenage or preteen children's actions belong anywhere along the continuum of adolescent rebellion from the not-so-serious to the very serious. The book is based largely on the principles of Families Anonymous (FA), a self-help group whose members around the country are parents of troubled young persons. In my work as a writer specializing in family problems, I've had extensive opportunity over the past few years to talk to FA parents in various parts of the country, and I'm impressed by the way these principles have helped them cope with painful problems related to their highly rebellious children. I've also invited suggestions from a number of very skilled mental health professionals who work with teenagers and their parents. These principles and suggestions may enable you to:

• Look more calmly and objectively at your adolescent's rebelliousness; perhaps you're worrying needlessly.

• Alert you to danger signals that indicate the opposite— that show the rebelliousness is more than "just a phase."

• Become less anxious about the situation, regardless of how worrisome it is.

• Relieve you of unnecessary guilt, that immediate reaction parents inevitably have when things go wrong with their children.

• Uncover ways in which you may be unwittingly encouraging destructive rebelliousness.

• Accept the fact that, however concerned you are about your children, your own well-being is just as important.

WHEN PARENTS COMPARE TROUBLES

Shortly after their daughter Jane turned fourteen, Bill and Trudy became so harassed they were convinced that nobody else in the whole wide world was going through their problems. The girl had been an excellent student; now she was barely paying attention to her studies. Hitherto cooperative, now she rebelled against the rules and regulations that she'd accepted as a way of life. She began to dress sloppily, often came home late for supper, refused to clean her room, and argued with her parents about every little thing—or so it seemed.

Truthfully, Bill and Trudy couldn't say she was doing

anything so terrible—except once, when she and a couple of girl friends were caught shoplifting some blouses. But she was so argumentative, so hostile, there were so few times when the lovable Jane they knew broke through the wall of anger and dissatisfaction she'd built around herself. Often the hassles began early in the morning, when Trudy had the thankless task of rousing the adolescent from her bed, and didn't end until nighttime, when she reacted with tantrums to pleas that she turn her stereo down. Bill and Trudy were exhausted. They were also embarrassed because their neighbors in this quiet, suburban, middle-western community were starting to make remarks about Jane.

When they met George and Myra, though, they felt better; their own circumstances were trifling in comparison to what those two were going through. George and Myra's older daughter, Annie, had also changed drastically soon after her thirteenth birthday. Her first teenage indication of rebelliousness was rudeness—she became unaccountably rude to both her parents and her teachers (who now complained that she was trying to boss them around). Her parents hoped Annie would grow out of it; on the contrary, her behavior grew steadily worse. When she was in the seventh grade they found evidence of marijuana in her room, though she steadfastly denied smoking it. When she was in the eighth grade she cut school a good deal of the time and was caught stealing perfume in a store when she had ten dollars in her pocket.

Lectures, pleadings, restrictions—nothing worked. Expressionless, Annie would simply reply, "Sure, okay," to her parents' entreaties, then go on doing her own thing. A week after the theft episode she and a group of friends broke some windows in her school. As for school, the eighth grade was a lost cause because she was truant so much of the time, and when she began ninth grade she was in school just twice the whole first month. At this point George and Myra decided to enroll their daughter in a private school. Annie didn't say much about this; she seemed passively accepting of the plan. But on the morning of her first day in the new school she ran away— and stayed away for three weeks, weeks that seemed like months to her unhappy parents. At last they found her, living in a commune in a seedy part of town. She came back as sullen and angry as she had left, lived with a relative for a while, returned home, and was making noises about running away again.

George and Myra were utterly despondent about the way Annie was ruining her life—and utterly alone as well, for none of their friends had such problem children. But then they met Ginger and Hal, after which they considered themselves comparatively lucky. Ginger and Hal's problem was their seventeen-year-old son, Sidney. They described Sidney as having been "a fine boy, an average student, neat and nice." That was so, they explained, until he got into the ninth grade, at which time he was introduced to marijuana. About then, much to their dismay, he let his hair grow long and gathered it into a ponytail. He practically stopped going to school and began to spend his time in the park with a bunch of young "parkies" roughly his own age—boys and girls who had also given up on school.

That was only the beginning. Sidney was arrested for possession of marijuana and, at the judge's recommendation, agreed to go to a psychiatrist. He went for six months; then the psychiatrist told Ginger and Hal that drugs were Sidney's "fatal flaw" and that there was nothing at present that could be done for him. Close to eighteen by this time, Sidney moved out of his parents' home and got himself a laboring job that lasted just a few weeks. They weren't sure what he lived on after that; they believed he was dealing in drugs to support his own habit. He was arrested again, this time for selling drugs to an undercover policeman. Now he faced a jail term—living at home in the interim, a very confused and frightened young man.

Ginger and Hal had thought their torment unequaled—until they met Walt and Ellen and learned what life was like with their older son, Doug. Also seventeen, Doug had rebelled violently against all rules and regulations since he was fifteen. Violence seemed at the core of his being. Sometimes in a tantrum he beat up his younger brother. More than once he had slapped his mother, so hard one time when she refused to give him extra spending money that she was knocked to the ground.

When he was sixteen, Doug went to a psychologist for a few months, but the boy was highly resistant to "working" in his therapy, and the psychologist finally concluded he might be better off going to a school away from home. He was sent to a boarding school more than a hundred miles away, but kept getting into fights there and refused to do his schoolwork. Finally he was expelled.

Back home again, Doug became a heavy user of pot, alcohol, and other drugs. One night he took some "angel dust," technically known as phencyclidine or PCP, which is easily compounded, is readily available, and has the fearsome characteristic of sometimes inducing intense paranoid reactions. These have been known to lead to attempted or actual suicidal or homicidal acts, and so it was in Doug's case. He went berserk, destroying his room and mauling his younger sister. He had to be institutionalized and spent some months in a mental hospital. Home once more, he works steadily in an automobile tire factory. Sometimes his parents think he's quieter, but then his violent temper flares up and they brace themselves for what might be a disastrous explosion. They're afraid of him, and at a loss as to how to help him and themselves. He refuses to move out. He still smokes pot and drinks, though not as much as in the past. "Doug is the type of boy who turns against anybody who tries to help him," his mother sadly commented. "He doesn't think he needs help."

GAINING PERSPECTIVE

When parents' tranquillity—or at least their familiar day-to-day routine—is upset by a disruptive adolescent, they may react typically. It's typical to feel, "Nobody's going through what I'm going through." It's typical to feel, "How could things be worse?" It's typical to feel alone in the situation and to think in extremes. *Their* child is the surliest, rudest, laziest, craziest. *Their* lot is the most miserable of all. The more disturbed their child's behavior becomes, the more isolated and luckless they tend to feel—as if fate had singled them out for an especially malevolent turn.

Such reactions are partly owing to another tendency of parents whose children are extremely rebellious and troubled: Even in these let-it-all-hang-out times they try to keep the problem as much as possible to themselves. Some admit they're frightened to have *anybody*—friends, relatives, business associates, neighbors—find out, especially if the problem is something as serious as drug addiction. Rightly or wrongly, they think "outsiders" to the problem won't understand—will criticize them and hold them and/or their children in contempt. Unfortunately, the more they isolate themselves, the more their inner tension grows, since they are not availing themselves of the relief that comes with the airing of pent-up feelings. And, with no one to help their perspective on the situation, it tends to become increasingly distorted.

Actually, as the experiences of the various parents described above show, no matter what kinds of adolescence-related problems your family may be going through, you're not alone. No matter how horrendous or overwhelming your problems look to you at the moment, there's always a family around whose circumstances are similar or maybe even worse.

These points may seem facile; they may seem like forced attempts to minimize the seriousness of your own situation. In fact, however, to realize—*truly* realize—that you're not "differ-

ent," not set apart from other, luckier parents, allows you to
adopt a more realistic and comforting perspective.

This is exactly what often happens with mothers and
fathers who attend parent-focused groups like FA, where everybody is struggling with somewhat similar problems. A father in
Baltimore who was drawn to an FA group there because his
daughter was a chronic truant recalls his and his wife's reaction
to their first couple of meetings: "We came there shattered;
we ended up feeling that our problems were relatively minimal." And a Chicago mother whose drug-dealing son faced a
year in jail says of her first few FA meetings, "I took one look
around and saw people in much, much worse shape than I. And
they were laughing and talking and carrying on their lives."

Without a doubt, if you have a rebellious or troubled
adolescent in the family, coming to believe that you're not
alone is the first necessary step in making life easier and more
pleasurable.

2. Are Things Really So Bad?

"I take it as normal for an adolescent to behave for a considerable length of time in an inconsistent and unpredictable manner, to fight his impulses and to accept them; to ward them off successfully and to be overrun by them; to love his parents and to hate them; to revolt against them and to be dependent on them ... to be more idealistic, artistic, generous, and unselfish than he will ever be again, but also the opposite —self-centered, egoistic, calculating."

So wrote Sigmund Freud's daughter, Anna, herself a pioneering psychoanalyst, more than twenty years ago in a classic paper on adolescence. She wasn't referring to emotionally troubled youths but to ordinary, garden-variety adolescents who grow up to take their respectable, conventional places in society.

"If there's one word to describe adolescents, that word is 'excessive,'" observes psychotherapist Thomas H. Waner, who has counseled teenagers extensively in Los Angeles's San Fernando Valley. "They feel excessively, perceive excessively, think excessively, and experience excessively. They're overwhelmed with stimulation. They have impulses and feelings that are new and strange to them, that they have no conscious way to assimilate and put order to."

Waner, too, is not referring only to troubled adolescents. Some experts say that if adolescent excesses are committed during any other state of life, they might be deemed psychotic, while in adolescence they're part of the normal process of development. Why, then, if some adolescents are so extremely turbulent or rebellious, do many others seem to march through their adolescent years in fairly stable fashion? Not every professional adolescent watcher agrees that turmoil is an inevitable consequence in the period spanning the years from the end of childhood (puberty) to the beginning of adulthood. New thinking on this period—triggered by landmark studies of "normal" middle-class adolescents—those who don't, and don't need to, wind up as patients in psychotherapists' offices—show that plenty of young people do *not* rebel extravagantly. According to extensive studies by psychiatrists at the University of Chicago School of Medicine, conducted with a large group of teenage boys, there is some resistance to adult authority. Among these boys and their parents there were some unpleasant parent-child scenes during early adolescence—mostly when the boys were twelve or thirteen, and usually around such familiar issues as clothes, length of hair, study habits, and the like—but while this created some stress, these boys never seriously deviated from their parents' values and expectations.

Why do adolescents rebel at all? Why do they sometimes act so wildly and inconsistently? Because physical (hormonal) changes bring on a certain amount of agitation—and physical maturation seems to occur earlier and earlier; many girls of eleven are already menstruating. Because adolescents are caught between childhood and adulthood, wanting to be children still, safe and protected from the scary outside world, and wanting equally strongly to be adults, finally rid of the restrictions and containments of childhood. Such a conflict creates much inner tension in them and makes many a teenager seem like a whiny kid one day and a composed, mature individual the next. Mostly, adolescents rebel because that's how they cut the psychological umbilical cord that has kept them tied as children to their parents. They need to flex their maturing muscles, as it were, test their newly developed strengths, and declare their independence. It may take a hard struggle to separate from their parents and stand on their own feet, making their own decisions, learning to assume the roles and responsibilities of adulthood.

LOOKING AT THE BRIGHT SIDE

When mothers and fathers view their children's actions very blackly and bleakly, they may be seeing things as much worse than they necessarily are. When they do this, they may unwittingly overreact, prompting the children to overreact in turn, so that ordinary rebellion may be intensified or may actually turn into something worse. (Overreacting is discussed further on at more length.) Conversely, with a slight shift in emphasis, parents can view the same actions and events more positively, minimize friction, cut down on their own emotional wear and tear, and help keep adolescent rebellion at manageable levels.

So it is that what seems like mindless defiance—a boy's insistence on letting his hair grow long, for instance, or growing a beard against his parents' wishes—has some logic to it. It may be his way of saying, "I'm an individual. This is my hair and I have a right to make my decisions about it. In matters that are of no major consequence to anyone but me, and can't hurt anyone including me, please lay off." It's an important statement.

So, too, seemingly time-wasting activities can be learning experiences. Lots of kids like to "hang out"—at the corner drugstore, in the park, around the shopping mall. They also tend to stay on the phone for hours in seemingly aimless conversation. These things often upset parents and other adults, who think their children should be doing something more constructive with their time. Seen in a different light, such activities reflect adolescents' need to learn to function as social beings.

Consider a fairly typical adolescent trait—changeableness —and how it can be viewed negatively and positively. Yesterday, Mary's parents were delighted when she grandly announced that henceforth she was going to quit fooling around —for starters, she planned to enroll in a fashion design course and take yoga classes. Today Mary is back at the old stand; she didn't want to go to school in the morning and she's off playing frisbees in the park instead of burying herself in her homework. Yesterday, Ted was a passionate tennis player, showing real drive and talent; his father, no slouch with a racket himself, was already mentally making plans for his son's career in tennis. But now Ted's tennis racket is gathering dust in the closet and he has turned into a photography nut, snapping photos and haunting galleries every chance he gets.

Mary's parents, and Ted's, can view their children's inconsistency in one of two ways. They can take every pronouncement very seriously and then, when there's no follow-through or the enthusiasm doesn't last, take the attitude, "I can't count on that child of mine to follow through on anything. All charged up one day, all those good intentions forgotten the next. Will Mary (Ted) ever amount to anything?" Acting on their disappointment and anxiety, they can also talk to their children about the changeability they perceive as a problem—but such talk tends to bring on flare-ups and leads to nothing constructive.

On the other hand, they can see this changeability as part of the adolescent's search for a separate identity. Young people struggling to discover who they are and what they want to be "try on" all kinds of roles, manners, attitudes, ways of seeing and doing things, to find out how these fit, much as a person tries on new clothes to see how comfortable they are.

Your hitherto modest child may suddenly adopt an arrogant know-it-all posture, insufferably proclaiming all kinds of ideas—half-baked ideas to you—with fanatical fervor. You may grow more and more outraged as you listen, for what finally dawns on you is that you must either agree to the validity of those silly ideas or be relegated to the category of blathering idiot. Whether the issue being debated is the possible health hazards of marijuana or the worth of contemporary religion, some parents react with a great deal of anger. You may come to be less angry, however, if you keep in mind that here's superconfidence as cover-up: behind that arrogance hides a teenager who's actually very unsure of himself and his ideas. He fears that if he presents his ideas to these people, his parents, whom he loves and respects, they'd only laugh at him. Given his state of uncertainty, that would be intolerable. So he's the one who comes on very strongly, eager to pounce on them first.

Another thing: Adolescents grow at a dizzying rate in terms of their cognitive powers; those mental muscles of theirs need exercise, and right at home they have the perfect sparring partners—their parents, of course. So what may seem like argumentativeness may be only their impatience to test themselves in terms of thoughts and words.

As already noted, studies of "normal" boys show that in basic, important matters most teenagers and their parents are in accord. At times the parents may not think so, may feel that, on the contrary, they and their adolescent children are in direct opposition on fundamental values. They may wonder with increasing gloominess if they'll ever see eye to eye again. But perhaps things aren't really so bad. A teenager's view of life can undergo startling changes from one month to another. Parents would do better to listen to their teenager without taking everything that's said too seriously. They are hardly hearing the child's final pronouncement. Many more will come—

quite possibly in direct opposition to each other.

What's more, parent and child may not be so far apart as things seem on the surface. Schoolwork is an example. A particular parent wants his child to study hard, get good grades, go to a good college, and earn a substantial living. The adolescent, though, says flatly that school is a bore. Are the two so far apart? Not necessarily. Most parents would agree with their children that there's no pleasure in learning for learning's sake, no pleasure in scholarship as an end in itself.

Another example: During the student protest days of the 1960s, many parents deplored their children's actions. They forgot whose children the rebels were—the parents themselves were mostly from liberal, professional backgrounds and had raised their boys and girls with a heavy emphasis on permissiveness and democratic participation. Such children find it hard to accept adult authority—so they assert themselves as their parents have taught them. Shared values.

Consider, too, that a seemingly irresponsible or self-destructive action on an adolescent's part may be the best reaction that child is able to give in the face of an unfortunate situation. For example, children in junior and senior high school all too often feel regimented, talked at by their teachers in a deadening atmosphere rather than intellectually stimulated. They feel this way because they are, in fact, regimented, talked at, in a dull, deadening atmosphere. Many youths are able to tolerate the boredom, to play the game. They attend school, go through the motions, and are there in body if not in spirit. Some young people can't adapt so well, can't play the game. Sooner or later, as they find the situation becoming more and more intolerable, they start cutting. It's not only a protest but a way of saying, "I want something that's better, healthier for me."

Here again, parents have a choice of looking at their children's actions negatively or positively—as proof of their adolescent irresponsibility or as legitimate protest. If they choose the former, they're likely to scold and punish their hooky-playing children, which only encourages more intense rebellion. If they choose the latter—to accept the protest as legitimate—they can help with exploring possible alternatives. At least they will have shown themselves empathetic and understanding as parents—qualities that in and of themselves help to reduce rather than aggravate adolescent rebellion.

THE HAZARDS OF OVERREACTING

When parents regularly interpret their adolescent's behavior in a negative way, even though that behavior isn't so alarming or could even be viewed in a positive light—when their reaction is excessive out of all proportion to its cause— they're overreacting. When they react to a mildly rebellious act as though their child is already sliding downward to ruination, they're overreacting.

"Some parents are quite frightened of rebellion," notes Nat Yalowitz, Director of Geller House, an adolescent residential center in New York City. "They immediately anticipate very serious consequences. Take the child who always comes to dinner with his hands washed, always goes to bed on time, always does his homework. The first time that child fails to do his homework his parents already see him going down the drain."

Unfortunately, what the overreacting parents fear often comes to pass, for parental overreaction is likely to spark the teenager or preteen to overreact in turn—that is, to escalate ordinary rebellion into the kind that really is worrisome. As Yalowitz puts it, "Parental overreaction becomes a self-fulfilling prophecy."

Beyond such unfortunate consequences for their children, mothers and fathers who overreact with needless alarm and anxiety are being unfair to themselves. Legitimate concern for their children's safety and well-being gives parents enough worries in the best of situations; excessive concern has a corrosive effect on their own well-being, for no one who is always on guard, always anxious, can enjoy life at the same time.

Here are five specific behavior patterns that overreacting parents habitually fall into:

They're extremely anxious generally about what's going on in their children's lives. They worry about sixteen-year-olds as though they were six—repeatedly caution them about the dangers of the world, question them closely about their activities, and one way or another convey, "I don't trust you, I don't think you're mature or responsible enough."

They're especially nervous about some one aspect of their children's lives. In the case of teenage daughters, sex is often it. A mother will stay up waiting for her adolescent girl to come home from a date and then grill her about the evening's happenings. A father will become terribly upset if his daughter arrives home as much as fifteen minutes late when she has been out with a boy; he imagines that wild sex prompted the delay. Again, what's communicated is, "I don't trust you," and so forth.

They generalize from a specific incident—exaggerate its meaning. Back to the example of sex again: A mother and father discover that their sweet little girl, their sixteen-year-old, has been having sex with her boyfriend. Panicked and angry, already seeing her as sexually promiscuous, and degraded, they call her a whore. Another example: A couple discover a pipe for marijuana in their teenage son's room. They scream and yell and carry on; in their outraged minds, their son is already a drug addict. A third example: A boy of fourteen is caught for the first time stealing some candy bars from a local supermarket. His heartsick parents act as though he's practically ready for the penitentiary.

They're always suspicious and ready to accuse. Whether the issue is sex, drugs, theft, or anything else of a potentially

serious or explosive nature, they don't ask or wait for explana-
tions. As soon as something arouses their suspicion, their extreme anxiety prompts them to see it as fact, and they are ready
to indict the suspected child.

They're quick to become very angry with their child. That
anger may be triggered by something the child does or says, or
even by a particular look or tone of voice. One father says he
finds himself enraged every time his teenage daughter adopts
a particularly snotty tone when talking to him, even if what she
has to say isn't itself offensive.

Parents who have a tendency to overreact may find it
helpful to understand just why their boys and girls become so
disturbed by this pattern of parental response. Like adults,
children become upset by treatment or accusations they know
to be unfair. Like adults, children are understandably aggrieved
when they perceive they're not trusted—all the more so, of
course, when they know there's no sound basis for that lack of
trust. Like adults, children are outraged when a relatively
minor infraction is treated like a major crime—outraged by the
unfairness of it all. And there's a greater reason. No matter how
vehemently they may deny it, young people do have a deep
need to see their mothers and fathers as strong and competent,
as being in control of themselves and of situations. When
instead they're confronted with a parent who habitually over-
reacts, yelling and screaming, they see a parent who isn't in
control. Given their own adolescent problems with control,
this is very unsettling to them.

As for the ways in which parental overreaction intensifies
young people's rebelliousness, they're showing their anger at
not being trusted or treated fairly. If they've been unfairly
accused or punished, they often feel, "If I'm going to be
blamed anyhow, I might as well go ahead and do it." And they
may, on a deeper level, have a need to test and retest their
parents—to see whether those overreacting mothers or fathers
will react more maturely and rationally the next time or the

next time, making the world a safer place for them again.

To help parents who are prone to overreact in relation to their children, family counselors suggest the following:

• When you feel a wave of anger toward, or anxiety about, your child surge over you, consciously will yourself to back off. Avoid saying or doing *anything* just then; first give yourself a chance to cool off or relax a bit.

• If you're especially worried about a specific situation, try —really try—to get as much information as possible. Parents often overreact on the basis of scanty data, tending to fill in the gaps by assuming the very worst. Don't jump to conclusions.

• Remember that children are entitled—no less than persons being tried in a court of law—to be presumed innocent until found guilty.

• In talking to the adolescent, especially in asking questions, be as cool and calm as you possibly can. Avoid judgmental questions—accusations in disguise. (Such questions usually begin, "Didn't you . . . ?" or, "Weren't you . . . ?")

• Try to retain a sense of proportion. The occasional marijuana smoker is *not* a drug addict; the girl sexually involved with a young man is *not*, on that account alone, headed for a sexually promiscuous life; the young person who's caught stealing once or twice is *not* destined for a life of crime.

• At the same time, if the child engages in antisocial behavior or otherwise does something of which you strongly disapprove, make that fact known. Make it known as calmly, clearly, and firmly as possible. This also holds true for values you want to share and rules you want to establish. Share the values and impart the rules as calmly, clearly, and firmly as you possibly can. Heated lectures, the hot-under-the-collar-I'll-drum-some-sense-into-you approach, incur nothing but resentment; the child on the receiving end perceives them as an assault. Whether the parent-child relationship has been satisfactory or is already troubled, a heated lecture will do more harm than good. Conversely, a firm and unambiguous statement of your position should either maintain a relationship characterized by mutual love and respect or help to repair a troubled one.

3. "Just a Phase"—or Is It?

How Parents Deny

Let's look again at the story of George, Myra, and daughter Annie in Chapter 1; it illustrates clearly, if sadly, another parental extreme—*denial.* When at thirteen Annie became disruptive in school and was also caught smoking cigarettes, George and Myra put it down to "puberty and all that jazz." They treated the incident casually, didn't say much to Annie about it. They assumed she would grow out of this rebellious stage.

When Annie became even more hostile and imperious the following year, both at home and in school, her parents commiserated with each other about the "terrible teens," gritted their teeth, said it was "just a phase," and knew she would straighten out soon.

Finding pot in her room when she was a seventh-grader, they told themselves that it must belong to one of her friends; *their* daughter would never be a marijuana smoker. They "discussed" the matter with Annie, giving her a lecture on the dangers of pot, and assumed that that would take care of things. When it became apparent that she was smoking a lot of pot, cutting school often, and otherwise getting into trouble —there was that shoplifting incident, for example—they had another long discussion with their daughter. "I was still in the position that it might happen to other children, but it could never happen to mine," Annie's mother now says. "I thought we were discussing it, but actually I was doing the talking and she wasn't listening."

Annie went on to help vandalize her school, became increasingly truant, and smoked pot even more heavily. All this precipitated more lectures, more fights, more screaming back and forth between parents and child. But it wasn't until Annie ran away that her mother and father at last said to themselves, "The situation is very serious."

WHY PARENTS DENY

If overreaction to minor problems is at one extreme point on a continuum of possible parental responses, denial of the seriousness of an escalating situation is at the other. Denial is a very human reaction. Everybody denies reality now and then as a form of emotional self-protection. When it comes to certain aspects of the human condition—death, for instance—denial is a universal characteristic; if it weren't, life would become unbearable.

Denial in parent-child relationships—when parents consciously or unconsciously avoid dealing with clearly troubling behavior on a child's part—is something else again. In the face of rebellious behavior on a child's part, mothers and fathers can comfort themselves with the hope, "It's just a phase," or "He'll get over it soon," or "She'll grow out of it before long." And often, most often, the hope is well founded; that's just how it works out.

Sometimes, though, it doesn't. A repeating pattern of behavior that indicates persistent emotional trouble in a child won't disappear of its own accord. Unless attended to properly, it's apt to worsen.

Yet many parents avoid dealing with it forthrightly and at a fairly early stage. There are many reasons for this. For one thing, it may be that the parents are very sensitive to the particular problem, and confronting it is too threatening to them. On the other hand, they may see it as overwhelming—as more than they can cope with. Then again, merely acknowledging its existence may make them feel like failures as parents. Some parents have a hard time in general dealing with harsh reality; whenever anything unpleasant occurs they're prone to duck the issue. And some others tend to think "magically"—for example, "If I don't acknowledge the problem, maybe it will just disappear." Another way is to think, "It just can't happen to us."

But, unfortunately, it does happen. For a variety of causes—which may have little or nothing to do with what's going on at home—some children do become emotionally troubled. They do become junkies and runaways and dropouts from school (and life), causing themselves and their families untold misery. Some do wind up in jail or have experiences that scar them emotionally or physically for life. And some children do, unfortunately, suffer from mental illnesses or neurological defects whose manifestations may first show up, or show up most strikingly, in adolescence. Among a small group of adolescents, schizophrenia is one important example.

Adolescence is also the time when a child with hitherto undiagnosed learning disabilities may become a serious behavior problem—in reaction to feeling so frustrated at not being able to learn as well or easily as the other students. Ann Chase, Director of the Adolescent Unit of the Family Service of Prince Georges County, in Maryland, says that 80 percent of the boys and girls referred to her unit have some form of learning disability. "Frequently these kids have at least average intelligence, so they're able to compensate and slide by—but they clown around and act impulsively, and that impulsive behavior is what's zeroed in on rather than the total picture," she says.

So parents have a hard job to do when their adolescent sons or daughters are being rebellious—not to become unduly alarmed and overreact, yet not to shrug off what could be a more serious problem, and, whatever the situation, to be quietly sensitive and alert to their children's actions and reactions.

DANGER SIGNALS

Obviously, most mothers and fathers are not clinicians, trained to discern the difference between normal behavior appropriate to a particular stage of development and behavior that's suggestive of the need for professional intervention. For that matter, as Anna Freud wrote in the paper quoted from earlier, even highly trained clinicians may have difficulty correctly diagnosing adolescent rebellion as normal or pathological.

Nevertheless, there are some warning signs and signals that can help alert parents to the possibility of a problem—the possibility, for instance, that the children in question may be dealing with a far greater load of emotional stress just then than they can adequately handle. Such signs and signals usually take the form of relatively extreme *changes of behavior*. For instance:

·The young person has been a good student, a better-than-average student. Now she has lost interest in school, neglects her homework, and is becoming increasingly truant.

·The young person has been outgoing and agreeable. Now he becomes sullen and withdrawn, stays in his room a good deal of the time, doesn't want to see friends, and loses interest in the hobbies and sports he formerly engaged in.

·The young person got along reasonably well with adults. Now she is hostile and troublesome with adults—especially so-called "authority figures" like parents and teachers; her relationship with them deteriorates.

·The young person hasn't used drugs, or, if he has, he confined himself to casual, experimental use (maybe smoking a joint or two over the weekend). Now his drug use increases dramatically.

·The young person has been fairly cooperative insofar as parental rules and regulations are concerned. Now she chafes at all parent-originating restrictions and blatantly defies their authority whenever she can. She insists they can no longer tell her what to do in any shape or form.

·Possibly portending an actual runaway episode, the young person stays away from home as much as he can, sometimes comes in very late at night, and occasionally stays with a friend all night long while "forgetting" to tell his parents where he is.

·The young person has had a number of friends her parents accepted as nice, decent kids. Now she calls these kids "straight," and wants nothing more to do with them. Instead, she spends her free time with new pals who are like her in defying adult authority and seeming to have no goals or ambitions.

Does your adolescent son or daughter seem to be going through one or more of these changes? If so, you may wonder how you can distinguish between signs of quite normal adolescent rebellion and warnings of more serious trouble. After all, many young people lose interest in schoolwork, say, prefer to remain by themselves, become particularly disagreeable to their parents, or briefly ally themselves with friends their parents consider undesirable. None of these acts needs to mean anything more than ordinary rebellion.

The difference is one of degree, of duration, and of the multiplicity of behavior changes. These are the questions you should examine: How long has this troublesome behavior been going on? Is the problem getting worse? Is it being compounded by other troubling acts on the child's part? As an example, take the early-adolescent boy who starts to become truant. If he occasionally plays hooky, it's a simple, fairly innocuous way of defying adult authority, of being the adolescent rebel. If he persistently cuts a particular class, there's more to it—there's probably something going on in that class he's having trouble with. If he is truant from school all day long, for a week or more at a time, it's certainly something that bears looking into. Maybe something about that particular school is now troubling him. Maybe something else in his life is troubling him greatly and this is reflected first of all in his attitude toward school. (When youngsters are under a good deal of emotional stress, it frequently shows up first of all in their schoolwork.)

If this boy stays away from school a lot of the time *and* seems draggy much of the time (an indication he may be zonked on pot or other drugs) *and* is turning hostile and secretive *and* has been dropping his straight friends, this escalating set of clearly self-destructive actions does at the least indicate a child who, just then, is under intense emotional stress. Parental concern is definitely called for, and action is needed. But what kind of action?

There are several steps that can be taken. Let's suppose the boy discussed above is your son. First, try to have a quiet talk with him. Depending on what it is that's troubling him, as well as on the degree of trust and sharing there exists between the two of you, he may open up. He may wish to speak to the other parent, or to both of you. (Respect that wish.) If he does tell you what's wrong, it's a very good sign. It means he hopes his mother or father (or both) will listen understandingly and help him try to work out a solution to the problem.

If he doesn't want to talk about it or practices his own brand of denial ("There's nothing wrong, Mom, you're making a mountain out of a molehill") you can encourage him to talk to some other mature and understanding adult.

In connection with school-related issues, it's possible that you would find it useful to confer with the school's guidance counselor. (Unfortunately, too many guidance counselors are both overworked and lacking appropriate skills to be truly helpful when there's a sensitive problem involving one of their students.) Boys and girls sometimes cut particular classes because they simply can't grasp the subject matter or are in the midst of a personality conflict with the teacher, a conflict they can't handle.

You can take a careful, honest look at the home atmosphere to see if perhaps something is amiss, something that has become quite stressful to the adolescent. Are mother and father in the midst of some marital conflict? Maybe even discussing separation or divorce? Is there, or has there recently been, serious illness in the family? (One teenage girl began a shocking series of rebellious acts a few months after her mother had a mastectomy; such reactions are far from uncommon.) On the other hand, maybe there's something in the parent-child relationship that's upsetting, some aspect he finds it hard to talk about or hasn't been able to convey to you too well. Chapters 5, 6, and 7 may be especially helpful in this respect.

A consultation with a psychiatrist, psychologist, or social worker who has had considerable expertise in working with adolescents may be the most constructive approach. This is especially likely if the young person is rebelling in a variety of self-destructive ways. (See Chapter 16 for an explanation of the work that mental health professionals do with adolescents.)

WHY NOW?

A question asked by many parents whose children have, seemingly with lightning speed, become highly rebellious adolescents is "Why now?" Here's a boy or girl who was very nearly a model child, they say, an honors student, a Scout. Here were happy, cooperative youngsters. But now, at twelve or thirteen or fourteen or fifteen or sixteen, these wonderful children have suddenly changed, suddenly become so sullen and hostile and rebellious they hardly seem like the same person. Why did it happen so abruptly? Why now?

No one explanation applies in every situation. Sometimes a child's behavior suddenly does become very different in the early or middle years of adolescence; sometimes it just seems so. When change really is sudden, it can be a response to a suddenly changed family situation—for instance, separation or divorce. Or sometimes, without realizing it, parents react differently to children once they become adolescents—they tighten up, become much more strict, precipitating an explosion of rebellion on the child's part.

Counselors say, however, that in many instances life at home hasn't been as rosy as the parents believe it has been when they first describe what seems like a sharp difference in the way their children are behaving. Could be the child has been changing for some time and the parents, unconsciously denying the problem, haven't noticed. As Dr. James Gordon, a psychiatrist at the National Institute of Mental Health, puts it, "Parents often say a child's so much worse, but it's more a matter of degree than of startling change. They're suddenly noticing."

On the other hand, the change could be sudden in that only now, with their newfound adolescent power, do some boys and girls dare to express whatever pain or rage has been seething inside them for some time—express it in a lacerating wave of rebellion. But why the pain? Why the rage? Whatever it is that's troubling them, at home or elsewhere, they haven't let it surface directly. Like their parents, children also deny reality at times when it's too hard for them to face.

YOUR SELF-HELP
PROGRAM

4. How to Cope with Guilt Feelings

Too Little and Too Much

The more seriously rebellious the adolescent becomes, the more anxious, angry, and guilty parents tend to feel. Guilt, that most human of emotions, is an inevitable—and often corrosive —element in the lives of families in crisis because of their children. Aware of it or not, acknowledging it or not, the adolescents feel guilty for causing their families all that grief. Yes, underneath it all, they really do. And, whether or not the parents are aware of it or acknowledge it, they can't help but feel guilty, too, in these circumstances. They feel accountable —at least, that the world holds them accountable. It's *their* children, the children they gave birth to or sired, the boys and girls *they* mothered or fathered, the offspring *they* raised, who are now drug-befuddled, or who have now given up trying in school, or who have run away from home, or who otherwise act in deviant or antisocial ways.

But some parents suppress all guilt as some others deny the existence of a problem even as it comes knocking on the door in the form of a truant officer or policeman. These parents say, "*I* wasn't the one who ran away," or, "*I* wasn't the one who stole." Or, "It isn't *I* who has been selling and using drugs." Or, "It isn't *I* who stopped studying and flunked all those subjects." They focus on their offsprings' actions as though these are occurring in a vacuum—as though their adolescent children are living lives totally unconnected, emotionally or physically, to themselves.

This phenomenon is often seen in runaway houses—certified shelters where some boys and girls who split from home go for a free roof over their heads. When their parents come to get them, youth counselors at the shelters attempt to engage the whole family in family therapy, the idea being to try to prevent a repeat runaway episode after the runaway returns home. When mothers and fathers cooperate in family therapy, what they typically want to do is talk *only* about the runaway act itself; as much as they can, they avoid going into the reasons why their children left home in the first place. To zero in on that aspect might uncover problems at home, might make them feel they'd failed as parents. They don't want to have to deal with the guilt this feeling of failure would produce—guilt that would, they believe on some level of consciousness, overwhelm them.

To deny its existence is one extreme way of handling guilt; to take on more guilt than could possibly be yours, even if you were in the very unlikely position of having done everything wrong as a parent, is another. There seem to be many more mothers and fathers who inundate themselves with guilt than those who disown any vestige of it. Some such parents don painful guilt even if their children's acts of rebellion are comparatively mild, for overreacting to a situation involving one's child and then taking on a wholly unrealistic load of guilt about it go hand in hand. But a large number of parents whose teenage or preteen children's rebellion is far from mild also burden themselves with a great deal of unnecessary, hurting guilt. They say (and think), "It's all my fault."

In fact, they feel so guilty they spend days pacing the floor, nights tossing and turning sleeplessly in bed; they hammer accusations at themselves and become so drained, so exhausted physically and emotionally, that they're close to being paralyzed. They can't seem to make decisions. They can't seem to act—especially in relation to the children who are causing them so much heartache. It's almost as if, by overburdening themselves with guilt, they don't *have* to act—as if they're saying, "I feel so guilty I'm utterly helpless. There's nothing I can do to help myself or to help my child." Guilt, in such instances, keeps them from having to face those painful issues, and from making torturous but necessary choices.

"IF ONLY" AND OTHER FALLACIES

One way guilt feelings work in parents is in leading them to agonize over the things they might have done—or not done —to prevent the difficulties their children are having. This was strikingly illustrated in the Minneapolis–St. Paul area recently at a group meeting of mothers whose sons and daughters had run away. One mother said, "I stayed home and hovered over my child. I should have been in the world more, gone to work —then maybe she wouldn't be the way she is now."

Another mother said, "And I've been thinking, 'If only I hadn't gone to work—if only I'd stayed home and been a real mother to the child—none of this would have happened."

A third said, "We married so young, we had a child so young, if only we'd waited awhile, been more mature—we'd have been better parents."

And still another said, "My husband and I always thought all the problems stemmed from the fact that we had this child so late in life."

Edna, a San Diego mother whose daughter has been a three-time runaway and also jailed for brief periods, recalls the way she whipped herself: "I kept asking myself, 'Where did I go wrong? How could I have failed so badly as a mother?' I'd always tried to be a good mother, always tried to do all the things we learn that we're supposed to do as mothers. But then I thought, 'Maybe if I'd given her ballet lessons when she was five, maybe if I'd agreed to be her Girl Scout leader . . .' Once I was asked and didn't have the time . . ."

"If only," prompted out of guilt, at least seems to give parents a handle, a bit of sense and logic in what would otherwise seem like a senseless tragedy. But since highly rebellious, disturbed children come from a wide variety of backgrounds— backgrounds that are not only different but sometimes in direct opposition to each other—sense and logic don't really apply. More importantly, observes psychotherapist Jan Robinson, in private practice in Minneapolis, when parents feel they could have changed things dramatically for the better if only they'd done this or that, they assume a kind of power they simply don't possess. When guilt feelings become so potent, she adds, "that particular child has become a reflection—the mirror image—of the parent. Then, when the child's in trouble, it literally feels as though it's happening to the parent."

Fact: No matter how much love and concern you feel for another human being, no matter how much you may want to protect that being, that child of yours, your responsibility for him or her is limited. It is limited by the fact that you are human, not superhuman, and that your child, too, is human— that is, far more complicated emotionally than to be the outcome solely of your influence as parents.

Factors Outside the Home

In primitive societies, the so-called "rites of passage" led children ritualistically into the teenage years. Anthropologists say entry into adolescence was so carefully structured because the older members of the tribes wanted to be sure the young people, with their impatience and their newfound power, wouldn't upset the established order of things. Today there are no rites, and families are very small. Aunts, uncles, and grand-parents don't live with parents and children in the same house, generally, as in times gone by, when these other family members took some of the pressure of child rearing off the parents. Now, often, the whole burden is on the parents—and in isolated bedroom communities, at that. Churches and social clubs are no longer the supports they once were, while male and female roles have become increasingly blurred, causing confusions all up and down the family line. Beyond these factors, with complex technology changing as rapidly as it does, parents no longer necessarily even have the authority of knowing more than their children, while equally fast-paced social changes frequently leave parents bewildered as to what's right and what's wrong.

Mothers and fathers aren't trained to be parents even in the traditional sense, much less to meet the demands of the day —for instance, to be able to give their children some sound drug education. Still another problem is that many, too many, schools fail to inform parents promptly when their children are truant. A number of outraged mothers and fathers, especially in southern California but elsewhere as well, tell of children being out for twenty, thirty, even forty or more days without their being notified.

INBORN TEMPERAMENT

Whenever anything has gone wrong with a child emotion-ally, the parents immediately get the blame. That's the way most of the psychological community operates and that's what has become ingrained in the public consciousness. So when things do go wrong, it's all the easier for parents to feel terribly at fault. But new research studies clearly show that the issue of blame—or responsibility—is far more complicated than that. While it's true, for instance, that a great many young drug addicts can fairly be viewed as having been emotionally deprived by their parents, that doesn't explain the fact that huge numbers of equally deprived young people never become hooked on drugs or otherwise commit antisocial or very self-destructive acts.

What makes the difference? Or, as the father of a seventeen-year-old mainliner put it, "Why was my kid cursed with this thing and not the kid next door?" Nobody knows for sure. Maybe one answer is "genetic weakness," that is, an inherited predisposition. Maybe several factors are involved, including the genetic factor in combination with the way this particular child was raised.

Some striking studies of very young children, conducted by Drs. Stella Chess and Alexander Thomas and various co-workers of New York University Medical Center, make it apparent that how parents relate to their children is only one important factor having to do with the way those children evolve. Chess and Thomas took a close look at newborn babies and then continued to observe them as they grew older. What they discovered primarily was that even the tiniest of infants comes into this world already possessing a distinct temperament. In fact, the two researchers found three well-defined kinds of temperament:

Easy children—have a positive approach to life; eat, sleep, and perform other bodily functions well; adapt well to new situations.

Difficult children—are intense; irregular in their bodily functions; tend to withdraw when faced with new situations; adapt slowly and are generally negative in their mood.

Slow-to-warm-up children—have a low activity level; are mildly intense; tend to withdraw when first faced with a new situation; are somewhat negative in their overall mood.

The significance of Chess and Thomas's findings is that when a child displays signs of emotional disturbance, it isn't simply because that child's parents "did something wrong."

What's wrong, often, is that the child's temperament actually clashes with his parents', with his teachers' (or with the structure of the school), with his peers'—or with all three.

Obviously, "difficult" children are the hardest to raise and account for the highest percentage of behavior disorders. Even the most skillful and sensitive of parents have a hard time with their "difficult" children. "Slow-to-warm-up" children may develop problems when their parents or teachers, acting in accord with their own temperaments rather than with the children's, push them to perform at a pace they are not suited to. And even an "easy" child may become difficult when his temperament is no longer in accord with his environment. For instance, many an easy child who has been raised to be a little individualist gets into trouble eventually when he resists the rigid demands of a conservative school.

This research may well explain why one child in a family becomes a behavior problem and the others not: The same parents who are relaxed and consistent with an easy child may become resentful, inconsistent, and rather helpless when raising the easy child's difficult brother or sister.

Insisting they don't find a one-to-one relationship between a child's disturbance and unhealthy parental influences, Chess and Thomas say, "Innumerable mothers have been unjustly burdened with deep feelings of guilt and inadequacy as a result of being incorrectly held exclusively, or even primarily, responsible for their children's problems."

Your Own Guilt

In the face of all these factors, you may nevertheless feel as did Jean, the mother of a violence-prone nineteen-year-old, a high-school dropout: "I know people who were treated very well by their parents who turned out like bums. I know others who weren't treated well at all and who turned out nicely. But

I still can't get out of my system the old refrain, 'Gee, look how bad that child is, he must have terrible parents.' "

Maybe that's how you feel. Maybe you're convinced you could have been more loving, patient, kind, tolerant, and understanding. Let's say you've made some mistakes as a mother or father—and what parent hasn't? As Ann Chase puts it, "I don't know of any perfect parents." Let's say, even, that some of those mistakes have been pretty serious. But are you really so powerful that you, single-handedly, have caused whatever painful events have come to pass? And what about other parents who have made similar mistakes, yet whose children never pop pills or steal or drop out of school? You cannot, alone, be held responsible for everything that goes on in your child's life, counselors stress, for there are too many other factors involved.

None of this is to suggest that you should simply gloss over your mistakes as though they hardly matter. They do matter, but ask yourself, counselors suggest, "Did I *deliberately* try to hurt my child?" The answer, of course, is no. Whatever you did, you did unknowingly, unwittingly, or because at the time you couldn't help yourself.

Jean, the nineteen-year-old dropout's mother, once nearly prostrate with corrosive guilt, learned that in order to go on living and loving and being a functioning wife and mother and all-round human being she had, finally, *to forgive herself.* "We did try. We weren't alcoholics or monsters. We didn't do anything on purpose to hurt him. We did it all with love, and it just didn't turn out right. You can only do so much. Everybody's human. Everybody has shortcomings."

5. Of Family Crises and Powerlessness

STAGES OF A PARENT-CHILD CRISIS

How does a crisis begin? Why does it heat up? When does it get out of hand? At Dale House, a runaway shelter run by the Young Life mission to teenagers in Colorado Springs, Colorado, Dr. James R. Oraker has charted the developing stages of a parent-child crisis.

Stage One. Paul and Kay vaguely sense that something is amiss with their fourteen-year-old son, Ted. He's not behaving as he used to. He's dropping his old friends in favor of kids his parents don't approve of. He's getting to look sloppy. He's not doing as well in school as he used to. His parents are concerned, but decide not to make a fuss at the moment. He's in puberty, they say; it will blow over.

Stage Two. Paul and Kay finally decide to say something to Ted; sometimes they punish him when he misbehaves and sometimes they don't; their attempts to deal with the situation are disorganized. Now they're worried about drug use; they ask Ted and he vehemently denies touching any drugs. They don't fully believe him, but they haven't any proof, either, so it's easiest just to let things go. But they do now keep lecturing him. Ted's conduct worsens, and his parents decide to crack down. They ground him, they insist he be home early in the evening, and they tell him what kinds of friends he may and may not have. They're into an escalating pattern of transgressions and punishments.

Stage Three. Ted's disturbing behavior becomes more open and outrageous. He pays no attention to restrictions or lectures and makes it clear in words and actions that they have no control over him. They talk about sending him to a psychiatrist, and at first he absolutely refuses to consider it. Finally, though, he agrees to go to a "shrink" of their choosing, "just to get you off my back," he tells them. But he doesn't really participate in the sessions, so nothing much is effected. Nothing except more problems, more conflict, more ill feeling on Ted's part toward his parents, and vice versa.

Stage Four. The full crisis is fast looming. With nothing resolved, with Ted hardly going to school and by now quite obviously heavily involved with drugs, Kay and Paul become more openly hostile, aggressive, and controlling than they had been. They lecture him constantly, threaten him constantly—to throw him out, to hospitalize him, to call the police. Ever defiant, Ted tells them to go to hell and, at fifteen and a half, runs away. A year and a half since its start, the full crisis is at hand. (In other situations, of course, this crisis pattern could take place over a few months or even weeks.) Paul and Kay feel utterly helpless.

PATTERNS OF HELPLESSNESS

If the pattern is familiar to many parents, so are the twin themes of helplessness and eventual hopelessness that run through the attitudes and actions of parents who see the crisis escalate out of control. They try everything. Scoldings, groundings, visits to therapists, attempts to enlist their children in drug rehabilitation programs, and so on and on—but nothing, not even the threat of court action against the child, works.

Still, as the weeks, months, and sometimes even years drag on, they continue to try, to search for some solution to the dilemma of their children's self-destructive actions.

Nothing seems to work, yet hope dies hard. Still, hope as they may, they find themselves growing more and more desperate. They can't concentrate. They lose their taste for food. In the latter stages of the crisis, sleepless nights are followed by days through which they pass like zombies. Many parents of extremely rebellious children, those who commit serious acts of delinquency, tell of losing, or being in danger of losing, their jobs as their every thought revolves around their self-destructive sons or daughters.

Says the mother of an eighteen-year-old boy who's now in jail for dealing in drugs, "When he was first taken away, I felt like I was the one trapped in jail. I wanted to help him—I wanted to solve his problem so much, and I couldn't—I couldn't."

In the case of a boy who stole money from his boss and threatened his girl friend with a severe beating if she told anybody he made her pregnant, his mother took to her bed for two weeks when she found out. She says, "I thought, 'I don't even want to wake up in the morning,' it was that bad. I mean, he was my child and it was like my arm was being cut off."

The mother of a runaway girl who was gone for six months without a single word recalls, "I just fell apart. This time I thought I was going to lose my mind. I was hysterical; I just wanted to go on crying and crying. I kept asking myself, 'What can I do?' but there was nothing I could do. I went to work, but a lot of the time I had to go to the bathroom and cry."

Paradoxically, it's at this point—the point of utter helplessness and nearly utter hopelessness—that real hope for the future can begin.

POWER AND POWERLESSNESS

Men and women often enter into parenthood thinking they'll always have adult power at their command, for that's how they (faultily) remember it from their childhood years. And for a while their expectations are fulfilled. But as their children slide into adolescence, parents lose a considerable amount of the power they once had. They're not so much stronger than their children now. They're not necessarily so much smarter or more sophisticated. In many respects their children are well able to take care of themselves, especially in contrast to when they were younger, and they derive many of their satisfactions outside the home, from activities with friends and peers.

In many instances, parents' loss of power is more than made up by the bond of love and respect that has been growing firmer and more durable over the years between them and their child. It's this bond—as much as or more than the parents' actual authority—that puts brakes on adolescent rebellion. The boys and girls may still test—and test and test—but they don't seriously challenge parental authority; they don't want to, don't need to.

In the case of highly rebellious young people whose acts are both distressing and destructive, parental power has little meaning. As Kay and Paul eventually found out, in the end it doesn't even exist. When Ted was younger, they could use parental power (authority) to control his behavior. As he grew more powerful in his own right—that is, less dependent on them for his survival—their power waned. Finally, there was nothing in terms of parental authority that they could do. Lectures didn't seem to penetrate his ears, much less to reach his mind. Punishments didn't work, either, for he circumvented them (he'd sometimes sneak out in the middle of the night, for instance, when he was grounded) or shrugged them off. Also, as the relationship between parents and son deteri-

orated, so did feelings of affection and respect. Ted went outside the home for these emotional needs—seeking them
among the boys and girls of whom his parents disapproved.

When parental power no longer works, when you've done
everything humanly possible, and your child, the child who's
involved in activities you deplore, no longer listens—when that
child of yours seems to offer little but rebellion and hostility—
when unhappiness hangs heavy over the family atmosphere
and you feel so tired and helpless and yet hope for something
more to do, somewhere else to turn, what then? Is there, then,
anything further you can do? Yes, there is. As many mothers
and fathers who come to their initial Families Anonymous
meetings discover, there is a first step toward a happier time
for you and possibly even for your child.

To take this step is at once very simple and very hard.
Simple because there's nothing to it except giving something
up; hardest because this "something" is one of the most tena-
cious and cherished set of beliefs parents hold. This set of
beliefs that you're asked to give up consists of:

•The belief that you can direct your child's life.

•The belief that you can change your child's life.

•The belief that you must, at whatever cost, continue
your efforts to protect your child.

•The belief that you have control over other people's lives
—your child's life and others'.

•The belief that as long as you have an ounce of strength
left it's your responsibility to continue to look for "solutions."

Instead, you're asked to admit that:

•You really are powerless to change your child's behavior.

•The crisis has reached the point where your life has
become unmanageable.

It takes a great deal of courage to make these admissions,
say parents who have gone through this painful but necessary
process. Yet they also say that, in retrospect, they were already
powerless long before they gave voice to the fact of it. And,

they say, they wish they could have come to that point much, much earlier, for it would have saved themselves, and in many instances their children as well, a great deal of heartache.

"If you try to make something work and it just won't, then you certainly don't have the power in that respect that you thought you had," explains the father of a teenage girl who ran away from her Ohio home and ended up a street prostitute in Manhattan's sleazy Eighth Avenue hard by 42nd Street. "If you're continually doing things to change your child's behavior and your child continues to act the same way, it's very obvious that you're powerless."

His wife adds, "When all these sad things go on, your own lives are going to have to become unmanageable. They have to become self-destructive when your youngsters are doing all of these things, and you're spending all of your time trying to find out where they are and what they're doing, and searching their rooms for drugs, and trying to find out who they're with, and all this kind of thing. It doesn't leave time or energy for anything else. You can't function as a person. You can't function as a wife. You can't function as a husband. What you have to do, once you realize your life is unmanageable, is to start putting it back into focus. Start concentrating on yourself, making your life a good, decent, manageable one that a youngster would respect. It's your only hope—for yourself and the child."

THE POWER OF POWERLESSNESS

It took Sheila and Pete a long time to give up the notion of parental power. But when they finally did, they discovered to their amazement that they were left feeling better, stronger, actually *more powerful* than during the agonizing years in which they clung to the belief that they could change their son's distressing ways.

Their long, unhappy time began when their son Roger graduated from high school at seventeen. To please his father, a retired naval career officer—and maybe to prove something to himself—Roger joined the Navy. But he was too shy, too sensitive a person for Navy life; very quickly he saw that it wasn't for him, and he felt wholly trapped and miserable. It didn't take him long, however, to find his escape—in the form of drugs. Speed and cocaine freed him from his misery; after a few months he compounded his problems by going AWOL for two weeks. He called his parents from Seattle, where he'd been hiding, and they flew there to retrieve him, broke and hungry and very scared. Because of Pete's intervention he didn't wind up in the stockade, but he was drummed out of the Navy with a less than honorable discharge.

That discharge prevented him from getting a decent job. At the same time, his mother pressured him to go to college and his father made it clear how badly his son had let him down. Frustrated, ashamed, angry, and self-pitying, Roger found refuge in drugs again. Deeper and deeper into the world of drugs he went, spending increasing amounts of time on the streets. Sometimes he disappeared for days, sometimes for weeks at a time. He had scrapes with the law. Once he was arrested for disorderly conduct, another time for passing a bad check.

The terrible events had a terrible effect on Roger's family, of course. His older sister worried so much about him that she nearly lost her job. His mother says of herself, "During all this time I screamed and yelled and stayed awake at night and became physically ill." There was a great deal of marital discord between her and Roger's father. She wanted Pete to do something to stop Roger from destroying himself; Pete wanted Sheila to do something. Neither knew what to do. They pleaded, scolded, threatened, begged Roger to enter a drug rehabilitation program, and generally put on all the pressure they could. None of it made the slightest difference. It was only when Roger was nineteen, temporarily living with a girl friend and as wretched as ever, that Sheila finally faced the fact that her life and her family's had become unmanageable.

Now she says, "You'd be amazed at how exhausting control is. You can just work yourself to death controlling, scheming, planning, and nine times out of ten it's not going to be any good at all. Once you admit to being powerless over other people's lives, over your own child, you no longer have to work yourself to death like that."

And she says, "When you hurt so badly, have lived through so much fear and anxiety, you feel very powerful when you realize you've done all you could; you can't do more. You feel very powerful when you come to the realization of your powerlessness—when you really believe it, it's like somebody has lifted the weight of the world off your shoulders."

But that, of course, is only the beginning.

6. The One Person You Can Change

WHO HAS THE PROBLEM?

Wanda is sixteen. She runs away from her comfortable middle-class home, plays house with her boyfriend in one of the relatively few hippie communes still left in this country, then hitchhikes to San Francisco and supports herself for a time working in pornographic movies. Is Wanda the problem in the family?

Fourteen-year-old Theresa, never an easy child, begins to have fits of anger, is nasty to her father and abusive to her mother, complains about everything, appreciates nothing that's done for her, refuses to do chores most of the time, and avoids eating with the family whenever she can. Is Theresa the problem here?

Barry, seventeen, becomes so enraged at his mother's refusal to lend him twenty dollars that he takes a valuable pearl necklace of hers and flings it out the window. Often, when he can't get his own way, he breaks something that doesn't belong to him. Is Barry the problem in the family?

Some parents, in all sincerity, have no difficulty answering such questions with a resounding *yes*. Yes, the acting-out children—the children whose destructively rebellious actions cause heartache to themselves and their parents—are definitely the problem. Some mothers and fathers, even when they're guilt-ridden and talking about the whole mess as being their own fault, still zero in on their children's misbehavior as though this is the only factor that counts.

After all, their children are the ones committing these actions, aren't they? This attitude shows up often in family therapy sessions in which parents and children participate at runaway houses, family service agencies, and in the offices of private practitioners. What the parents are eager to do—what they are at the session for—is to focus on their rebellious children. They want the professionals to change their children.

In fact, it's more than useless to point the finger of blame in any one direction, whether parents *or* children; it's unrealistic. When something goes seriously wrong in any way in a family—be it illness, loss of job, marital conflict, parent-child conflict, or other stressful situation—to greater or lesser degree everyone in the family is affected, in both feelings and behavior. To that extent it's everyone's problem, and no single person can be isolated as "the" problem, the culprit.

As psychotherapist June Toellner, of the American Institute of Family Relations in Los Angeles, says, "When a problem occurs in a family, it's not any one person's problem, it's a family problem."

This is a very important point to keep in mind, for it serves as a guide to the most logical and constructive directions that parents can follow, once they have become fully convinced of their powerlessness. After all, if it's all your fault, then your burden of guilt is overwhelming and thus prevents you from changing anything. If it's all your child's fault, you can't change anything either, since changing your child is what you've been trying to do unsuccessfully for so very long. If it's all the fault of anybody else around—your spouse, maybe, or your child's friends—you obviously can't effect change there, either.

Disturbances within a family are always so complicated

that to try to pin blame—or measure whose responsibility it is
—among the participants is futile. Everyone involved is
affected, everyone is a victim.

"Each person in a relationship has one hundred percent
responsibility for that relationship," June Toellner stresses.
"Each person, regardless of age, is fully responsible for himself
and for what happens to him in the family setting. When
there's a breakdown in the family it doesn't make sense to ask,
'Whose fault is it?' It could be everybody's fault and nobody's
fault. That means, when it comes to change, each person
involved has to take responsibility for himself."

WHY LECTURES DON'T WORK

Many mothers and fathers whose children are rebelling in
destructive ways don't understand why none of their lecturing
has any effect. They talk and talk and talk to their children
about the hazards of drugs, of alcohol, and it doesn't sink in.
They talk and talk about the importance of going to school, of
leading a decent life, and they're simply ignored. The more
rebellious their children become the more they lecture, and the
more they lecture, it seems, the more rebellious the children
become. Why? Psychotherapists who work with adolescents
explain:

•Lectures convey, "I'm the parent, I've got the power.
You'd better listen."

•Lectures convey, "I've got all the answers; there's nothing for you to say."

•Lectures convey, "I'm not interested in understanding
you or why you did what you did; your job is to obey me."

•Lectures make a child feel like an object rather than a
thinking, feeling person who deserves the respect of being
talked *with*, rather than *at*.

•By their very repetitiveness, lectures are a bore. Children who are often lectured soon develop the facility of tuning out.

· Perhaps the worst overall effect produced in children by repeated lectures is the feeling of what's-the-use?—the feeling that no matter what they say in their own behalf, they'll not be listened to. (End result of all the above: plain old resentment.)

Conversely, parents who finally do learn to stop lecturing and start listening say this has amazingly improved their relationship with their rebellious children. A father whose son finally ended up in a drug rehabilitation program recalls his first visit there: "I'd had plenty of time to realize how I'd lectured my boy and otherwise tried to take over his life. So when I went to visit Mike at the center, and he showed me around, all I did was to ask a few questions. I never once tried to think for him, or take over, or anything like that. Well, he wrote me a letter afterward, and it was the friendliest he'd communicated with me since before he reached his teens. In the letter he said, 'Father, this was the first time you've listened to me for years.'"

And this from Pete, whose son went AWOL from the Navy and also became a drug addict: "I'd lecture him; if he talked back I'd say, 'Shut up, I'm your father.' Now I try to understand his feelings and talk his language. Now we meet each other, say, 'Hi, guy,' and throw our arms around each other. If I forget and get on him for something, he'll say, 'Hey, guy, get off my back,' and that's okay. He's right, because I'll have been lecturing again. We like each other now."

WHY PUNISHMENTS DON'T WORK

Parents who repeatedly punish their adolescent children in some way—grounding them, cutting down on their allowances, not letting them use the family car, whatever—soon discover that punishment doesn't work, either, in controlling their children's actions. In fact, the more they punish, they find, the less constructive effect it has.

Ideally, punishment teaches children not to repeat the offensive behavior that triggered the discipline in the first place. Ideally, it teaches them to control themselves next time the impulse to behave that way comes upon them. Sometimes it works; with highly rebellious children it obviously doesn't or they would stop being so rebellious. Here are some reasons why it doesn't:

·The parents may be using punishment only because they feel angry, impatient, or helpless; children pick up such motivations very quickly, perceive the punishment as unfair, and become very resentful.

·In order to be effective, punishment has to be very consistently applied—that is, applied each and every time the child commits that particular offense. But that's impossible for most parents to do, and many are quite inconsistent. They punish or don't punish depending on their mood and level of toleration at any given time. This is a perfectly human response, but when children are sometimes punished and sometimes not punished for the same misdeed, they become confused and resentful—also a human response.

·The punishment may be excessive in relation to the misdeed; again, the child perceives it as unfair and becomes resentful as well as confused.

·Parents often don't realize that the more children are punished, the less able they are to relate cause and effect—to see exactly what they are being punished for. Instead, they associate punishment with the person meting it out; in effect, they think, "This parent is mean, therefore this parent punishes." The ostensible point of the punishment is completely lost.

·Highly rebellious children often have a great deal of trouble controlling their impulses, and simple punishment usually doesn't help them develop the inner controls they lack.

•Highly rebellious children know how unhappy they make their parents, even if they adopt an outward I-don't-give-a-damn pose. As a consequence they store up enormous amounts of guilt. The guilt produces tremendous inner tension; to relieve it, they want punishment. To get the punishment, they do something to bring it on. Thus, they misbehave, their parents punish, they misbehave some more, and the parents punish again, in a never-ending vicious circle that no one involved is aware exists.

TAKING YOUR OWN INVENTORY

When lectures and punishments don't work and nothing else that's been tried does, either, and when the fact is accepted that everybody in a relationship (including the parent-child one) has 100 percent responsibility for that relationship, the inescapable conclusion for each parent in this predicament is:

"The only person I can change is myself."

Consider it. To rack yourself with guilt is to cause yourself needless pain and do no good for others. To ferret out what everybody else involved has done that's wrong causes them needless pain and accomplishes nothing worthwhile. But to take a good look at yourself and your own actions and attitudes —without beating yourself over the head with recriminations —is to enter a process of growth that can't hurt and often has a tremendously positive effect on everyone concerned, including the rebellious youth.

That notion may sound good, but upon hearing it for the first time many parents, even those who have reached the point of admitting to powerlessness, resist it. They've been at the target end of angry, bitter, defiant children. They feel as if they've been through the wringer—and, of course, they have. They hurt badly. (Understandably, at this time, they forget how much their children hurt, too.) So the notion of changing themselves isn't one to which they respond with the greatest enthusiasm.

For instance, many if not most of the mothers and fathers who join FA groups at first balk at the idea of looking at themselves. They protest, "I'm not the one who's been causing all this suffering," and "I don't deserve to be treated this way." They insist, "I've tried so very hard to reach my child." But then they hear other parents who have broken through this resistance talk openly and candidly about themselves—hear them, in FA language, make a "searching and fearless" inventory of themselves.

Typically, a seasoned FA parent may talk about *false pride:* "Superficial things were so important to me," a mother says. "Now I've learned not to look for my children to do something to make *me* look good."

Another brings up *intolerance:* "I was brought up in a very strait-laced family where ladies didn't smoke and gentlemen didn't do this or that and they had a pigeonhole for everybody. So that's the way I raised my son—being intolerant, making judgments, putting him on the defensive all the time."

A third reveals her *suspiciousness:* "I was such a dishonest mother, you wouldn't believe. Pretended to trust Gloria when the truth is, I sneaked looks in her bureau drawer for 'evidence' and tried to get her locked diary open so she couldn't tell I was doing it. But I was always asking her pointed questions, too, prying into things, and she knew that my trust in her was zilch."

So, gradually, many resistant parents come to realize that opening themselves up to that "searching and fearless" inventory—acknowledging that they, too, aren't perfect—is another necessary step in the process of restoring their lives to a more peaceful state.

Here's how parents who have gone through the process say it works its magic:

•By concentrating on themselves as they take their own inventories, they stop focusing so intently on, and worrying so terribly, about their rebellious children. This takes the pressure off the children, which immediately has the effect of lessening parent-child tension.

•By easing up on such of their own negative patterns as they have recognized, they remove one or more factors that were helping trigger their children's increasingly rebellious and destructive acts.

•And a bonus, as one FA mother neatly put it: "It's a relief not to have to pretend to myself that I'm perfect any more!"

7. When Parents Look at Themselves

When parents look at themselves and at the ways in which they may have contributed to whatever frictions and tensions exist between themselves and their adolescent children, several major themes keep recurring.

Do any of them apply to you and your family situation? Read this chapter with an open mind. If possible, have your spouse read it, too, both of you alert to the possibility that some of the patterns described may, to greater or lesser extent, reflect similar patterns in your own family. A frank discussion between the two of you afterward may be surprisingly revealing.

One caution, however. If you and your spouse are having this talk, each of you should be sure to speak only of your own, not the other's, behavior. This kind of exercise easily lends itself to accusations and counteraccusations, especially in times of stress, and an accusatory stance can only cause more pain and anger. Conversely, looking honestly at yourself—accepting that you are the only person you *can* change—is the way to constructive change.

Many mothers and fathers have trouble letting their children grow up. Putting it another way, the fact that their children are on the brink of or already into adolescence can be very upsetting to some parents. It happens over and over again that the same parents who did such a great job of raising their young children falter when those same children turn twelve, thirteen, fourteen, or older. Without necessarily being aware of it, lots of mothers and fathers don't really want their offspring to become teenagers. They're made uncomfortable by that push toward adulthood, and there are several ways they show it:

• They make all kinds of decisions for their children that, at this stage of their development, would be best made by the children themselves. An extreme but not-so-uncommon example: the mother who still picks out her daughter's dresses, though the daughter is sixteen.

• They shelter their children as much as they possibly can from life's risks. Dotty's mother hovered over her when, as a child, she played on the swings in the park; she didn't want her to fall off and hurt herself. Dotty's father reacted with a great deal of nervousness when Dotty first learned to ride a bike; he was afraid she'd pedal out into the street, and there was a lot of discussion as to whether she'd even be permitted to have a bike. As Dotty grew older, both parents always prided themselves on knowing where Dotty was and whom she was with. They were not so much protective as overprotective. The older she grew, the more Dotty seethed at the way her parents were controlling her life; in mid-adolescence, then, she rebelled violently.

• They're always there to set things right when their children make mistakes. (Chapter 9 will deal more extensively with the importance of letting one's children learn from their own mistakes.)

• They set inappropriately strict rules for their children's life and conduct. Adolescence is the time when boys and girls are most anxious to strike out on their own, test their own beliefs, and determine their own life and future as much as they possibly can. This is important, necessary, highly appropriate "work" on their part. Yet this is the very time some parents clamp down hardest—on length of hair, clothes, curfew time, friends, smoking, cleanliness, the condition of their rooms, what they eat, schoolwork, and so forth. An inevitable parent-child power struggle ensues. With some justification, the children see the struggle as one for control of their lives, and sooner or later some will rebel against all parental rules and limits, the reasonable ones as well as the unreasonable.

It may help parents to see *what* they may be doing to impede their children's growth; it may also help them to understand *why* they're doing so. Family therapists point to one or more of the following reasons:

In terms of their skills and authority as parents, they may feel surer of themselves with younger, more helpless and dependent children. They doubt their own ability to handle, contain, control, negotiate with, or set limits for those "wild" teenagers.

Then again, it may be that in one way or another their own adolescences were disturbing. They might not remember the exact experiences that made them so unhappy—these are often suppressed from the conscious mind—but seeing their own boys and girls slipping into the teenage years stirs, however vaguely, disquieting remembrances. (These often relate to sex).

Some parents are acutely uncomfortable about growing older. In having to acknowledge their children's adolescence they're forced to face even more directly the reality of their own aging. To some extent they want to deny the exuberance, energy, power, and burgeoning sexuality they see or sense in their children. So, in a youth-worshipping nation, it's far from unusual for middle-aged parents who feel themselves on the decline to act upon the wish that goes, "Let's pretend they're still kids for a little while longer."

The irony is that the more parents try to control their children's lives—protect them from "bad outside influences," from physical harm, and from the other hazards of life—the more rebellion they encourage. As children grow older, they want and need to feel that their judgment is sound and to be trusted. The less they're allowed to use their own judgment—

and to learn from the experience if it turns out to be faulty—
the more resentful and rebellious they become. Then they feel
themselves justified in conning their parents, in using lies and
subterfuge to get more control over their own lives.

*Many mothers and fathers see their children as extensions
of themselves.* This is one of the easiest traps of all for parents
to fall into—simply by virtue of the fact that these *are* their
children, their flesh and blood, and also because they *have* all
these years been responsible for their well-being. It's the rare
parents, after all, whose minds haven't become a kaleidoscope
of colorful hopes and expectations for their child, from the
time it was born through its growing-up years—or longer. And
it's impossible for the parents, as they entertain such hopes and
expectations, to do so dispassionately—that is, free from their
own yearnings, their own unrealized dreams.

A parent will often think, "Well, I didn't, but maybe my
child will . . ." Maybe my child will be an outstanding student
the way I wasn't, become homecoming queen or a jock on the
football team as I wasn't, become the doctor I wanted to
become but didn't, be the financial success I wanted to be but
wasn't, marry the wealthy man or the beautiful and accomplished woman I didn't.

As children mature, as their own distinct personalities
emerge, some parents let go of those expectations and allow
their offspring to work out their own destinies. Others do not.
Many parents of highly rebellious adolescents, unknowingly
viewing them as extensions of themselves, show it by:

•Wanting their children to live up to the image they've
set up for them (which often involves impossibly high standards in relation to the particular child's gifts or inclinations).

•Rejecting their children (frequently showing anger disappointment, withdrawing love, and so on) when they express
their individuality in ways that don't conform to the parental
image of what they should be. This sometimes happens, for
instance, when a father has his heart set on an athletic star and

gets a bookworm instead, or when a mother wants her daughter to be a glamour puss and instead winds up with a child who couldn't care less about her looks or clothes.

·Finding it very upsetting when their children want to separate from them in a psychological sense—want, in the popular phrase "to become their own persons." The more parents gain their major satisfaction from their children, the more upset they are by these attempts at separation.

·Overreacting whenever their children get into trouble—going through paroxysms of shame as if they, rather than their children, committed the offending acts. "I wanted my daughter to be good for my sake, not for her own—and there's all the difference in the world," said one mother, a single parent with a repeat runaway daughter, ruefully explaining—at least in part—her daughter's need to rebel.

Many mothers and fathers make idle threats or are otherwise inconsistent in their child-rearing approaches. Frank's parents are an example. This eleven-year-old son of theirs likes to lean out of his bedroom window, on the second floor of the family's house, and shout down to his friends below. His father hates the racket and has an "ironclad" rule that Frank must never do that. And sometimes he does energetically clamp down on Frank when he hears him shouting back and forth with his chums, but at other times—as when things have gone especially well at the office and he's in a very good mood—he's indulgent and lets Frank get away with it.

Hilda, fifteen, has a habit of straggling in anywhere from fifteen minutes to an hour after the start of dinner. This is very annoying to Hilda's mother, and they have repeated arguments about the problem. Hilda's mother also repeatedly makes a pronouncement: "If you're late for supper, you get no supper —period." But sometimes, if the rest of the family is relaxed and joking at the dinner table, she lets Hilda join them even if she's late. And she never attempts to stop Hilda from going into the kitchen to eat leftovers or prepare something for herself, even if she's as much as an hour late in getting home.

Sam's parents are concerned about this thirteen-year-old's growing use of foul language. They keep telling him they're going to deduct fifty cents from his allowance whenever he swears. They did it twice; Sam set up such a howl that, though they keep threatening, they haven't done so again. And Sam keeps on swearing.

Kenneth's parents are furious with him whenever he cuts school; he's been doing that increasingly ever since he got into junior high school. They warn him that if he goes on cutting they'll deny him the use of the family car. Idle threats, so far —not once have they actually withheld the car keys from this sixteen-year-old.

Since she was five or six, Tanya had been in the habit of stealing coins from her mother's purse. Her mother knew it and gave her a few talks on honesty, but never gave away the fact that she was aware of Tanya's little acts of pilfering. She rationalized, "If I make a fuss, Tanya will see it as a big deal and either feel crushed or be angry with me and steal some more. She'll grow out of this thing." But when Tanya was eleven her teacher caught her stealing coins from *her* purse. The girl was forthwith sent to the principal's office. A call home was made, and Tanya was suspended from school for two days. Tanya's mother was furious—and grounded the girl for a whole week. Tanya's reaction: anger and confusion. She knew her mother had known about her thievery right along. Why hadn't she ever done anything about it before? Why was she only now punishing her?

When parents aren't consistent in the rules they make and the expectations they have, when they threaten punishments that are sometimes carried out, sometimes not, when, as in Tanya's case, they ignore a troublesome situation until they can't possibly avoid it and then crack down hard—then the children involved do become understandably angry and confused. They never really know where they stand with their inconsistent parents—and ambiguity, difficult for most people to handle, is especially hard on children and adolescents.

When they're on the receiving end of inconsistency in discipline and limit setting, many teenagers and preteens go on to test and test their parents. They feel the need to see if, eventually, they will get a consistent reaction, after all—a reaction that will make clear where they stand. And if they never get it, they will learn—eventually—not to take seriously *any* warning, threat, or parental definition of unacceptable behavior and its consequences.

Many mothers and fathers unwittingly give confused messages—"double messages"—to their children when they talk to them. This is another major source of confusion and anger in parent-child communication. A double message is, in effect, a combination of two messages that are in direct opposition to each other. Both can be verbal or, as sometimes happens, one is verbal, the other nonverbal. Here are several examples:

• Mother tells daughter, "I trust you"—then proceeds to question the girl closely about her friends and activities.

• Father tells the children, "Honesty is the best policy"—then cheats on his income tax or is underhanded in business.

• The parents berate their child for getting poor marks in school—but refuse to put him or her in the remedial classes the school has suggested.

• The parents criticize their child for having a lackadaisical attitude toward schoolwork—but also tear down the school's teachers and administrators as a bunch of incompetents.

• Mother generally conveys a fearful attitude toward life; when the kids are in their teens, for instance, she still claims she worries about their crossing the street, and so on—and yet she ridicules them if they panic when they have to take a test.

• Father tells his sons it's important for them to obey the laws of the land—then betrays a little pride when they get into trouble for stealing or committing vandalism. (He remembers doing the same when he was a kid—they're a chip off the old block.)

•Mother finds out daughter has been pilfering things when she's baby-sitting in people's homes and tells the girl this is the wrong thing to do—but, basically unable to come to grips with the situation, laughs it off as nothing serious.

•Mother tells daughter, "You're a beautiful girl; the boys will fall all over you; isn't that wonderful!"—and at the same time says, "Don't let them touch you."

•The parents say to their child, "We love you very much" —but also say (or convey), "Why can't you be more the way we want you to be?"

Like all faulty communication, double messages lead to trouble. They produce confusion and anger born of that confusion. Children who get double-messaged rightly feel, "I don't know what you want"; "No matter which way I go, I can't please you"; "Since you're being fuzzy about what it is you want, I'll do what *I* want."

Many mothers and fathers are too critical with their children. Typically, they don't mean to start out that way, and they may not have been so critical when their children were younger. (There may not have been that much to be critical about.) But as their youngsters become more rebellious as pre-adolescents or adolescents, and perhaps get more into trouble, they focus on the problems.

This is understandable. They're not used to rebellious acts and attitudes, at least not to the extent to which these are now emerging. They don't comprehend where all that negativism or outright hostility is suddenly coming from. They're perplexed as to why their sons or daughters should now be losing interest in schoolwork, or starting to play with drugs, or not minding family rules and regulations, or otherwise creating a lot of turmoil.

The parents know how easy it is for young people to get into trouble—serious trouble—escalating trouble. They're scared it will happen to their children. So they nag, lecture, complain, reprimand. They see this as a display of love, of their very genuine concern—and it is. Their children, though, see it as badgering and worse—and to a degree they're right, too. So they turn on the very people who have only their well-being in mind.

The circle of misunderstandings, miscommunication, and misinterpretations grows ever more vicious. Because of their apprehensions, the parents become overly sensitized to the possibility of wrongdoing, of antisocial and self-destructive behavior on their children's part; the children become overly sensitized to their parents' suspiciousness and watchfulness. Whether or not it's actually happening, they *feel* as if their mothers and fathers are forever checking up on them—reading their diaries, rummaging through their bureau drawers, keeping a ready ear cocked when they're talking to their chums on the phone, asking pointed questions, and otherwise invading their privacy.

The children feel keenly their parents' distrust, the apparent view of them as "bad." It tears them apart inside (though they'd be loath to admit it, even to themselves). In truth, as the family crisis worsens, the parents often do concentrate on the misbehavior as if their children really are all bad, devoid of redeeming qualities; they become so critical, so judgmental, without meaning to or wanting to, that there's no room left for praise. (Or what little praise they give is discounted by the children, who see themselves as the targets for so much censure.)

After taking stock of himself, one father in such a situation admitted, "We were so caught up in what Eddie was doing wrong, we forgot to say anything nice to him. And the more we did that, the more he had to prove us right." As long as such a high level of criticism is maintained, the hostility and rebellion aren't apt to lessen.

Many mothers and fathers unwittingly scapegoat one child

in the family. The scapegoated child is the child who's unfairly reprimanded or picked on for one reason or another and reacts to the situation in one of two ways—by withdrawing (avoiding contact with adults and peers to the point of becoming as much of a recluse as possible) or by vigorously rebelling.

Obviously, the vast majority of mothers and fathers don't want to be unfair to any of their offspring and don't mean to be, and it hardly ever even occurs to them that they are in fact engaged in the process of scapegoating. It just begins to happen and, after a while, becomes integrated into the family's interrelationships.

The scapegoat is the klutz, who's always breaking things; the one who always seems to get into trouble, who never seems to do anything right, who's labeled "different" from the other children because of his or her looks, mannerisms, or ways of doing things.

At times a parent unknowingly scapegoats a child because the child reminds that parent of something unacceptable within himself or herself. The awkward, klutzy child can be an example, as in the case of Max and his son, Burt. A highly skilled engineer, Max nevertheless was the unhandiest of men; he had trouble replacing as much as a burned-out light bulb. Max wanted Burt, his only son, to excel where he didn't, but Burt is no more accomplished with his hands than his father; if anything, he's even more awkward. So Burt became, and remains, the family scapegoat. "Anything he touches falls apart," his father jeers; his two younger sisters gleefully call him "dopey."

Sometimes, too, a child is unintentionally scapegoated by his mother and father when there's marital conflict in the family that the parents haven't yet been able to face directly. It becomes easier to see one child as the "problem," to focus on that child and make him their central concern. This allows them to avoid looking seriously at their relationship and its difficulties.

So it was with Lanie's parents. They were growing increasingly disenchanted with each other, but they were afraid to open up the situation, for it might lead to ugly scenes, maybe even to separation or divorce. Thus Lanie, their only child, became the peg on which they hung their dissatisfactions. Lanie was ideally suited to the role of scapegoat, since she wasn't an easy child to begin with. Her mother and father devoted themselves to worrying about her. She became the distraction that allowed them, quite without knowing what they were doing, to avoid facing each other. The more they worried about her, predictably, the more difficult and rebellious Lanie became, especially after she reached adolescence.

It's quite hard for parents who are unknowingly scapegoating one of their children to realize what they're doing. Still, there are ways they can at least consider whether the problem actually does exist within their families. If you want to find out whether scapegoating is going on in your family, answer the following questions as honestly as possible:

Is one child automatically targeted for blame if something is broken?

Is one child often the butt of family jokes?

Do you often wish one of your children would be very different from the way he or she is?

Is one particular child always getting into jams?

If the answer to any of these questions is yes, it's possible that this particular child is the family scapegoat.

Here is another exercise that may help you determine whether your rebellious (or withdrawn) child is also your scapegoated child. Make up a list of a dozen admirable personality traits, such as:

pleasant	vital	considerate
friendly	happy	sociable
helpful	resourceful	realistic
bright	humorous	open-minded

Use these or any other traits you believe to be important qualities in a child. Next to each of these traits jot down the names of those of your children who in reasonable measure possess these qualities. Now for the key question: Is the name of one of your children conspicuously missing from most of the list? That child is apt to be the scapegoated one.

After reading and reflecting on this chapter, do you feel that at least one of the patterns described characterizes you or your family situation? If so, becoming aware of its existence is a significant first step in eliminating it. Awareness may also lead you to feel suddenly very guilty—but, as Chapter 4 pointed out, everybody makes mistakes, no parent is perfect, and becoming immersed in guilt feelings keeps one from positive action.

Don't expect yourself to break the pattern all at once just because you know about it now, especially if it has been going on for some time. It may be that outside intervention, such as short-term counseling or family therapy, is the most constructive approach in working toward a change. But even without professional help you can help yourself to change. Much, of course, depends on how alert and aware you are in spotting the pattern each time it starts to recur—and on how determined you are, each time, to stop it right then and there.

Also, don't expect your child to alter his or her self-destructive behavior just because you're starting to do things differently now. This is a most important point to keep in mind. When parents go at self-change with the express aim of causing change in their children, their efforts are almost sure to wind up in failure. There are two main reasons for this. One, they're engaging in a kind of manipulative effort rather than acting on a genuine desire to alter their own negative patterns for their own benefit. Two, in effect they're telling their children, "See, I do things differently now, so I expect you to do the same"—which merely results in making the children involved feel all the more pressured.

On the other hand, don't think that your changes will go unnoticed. They definitely won't. Your adolescent's first reaction is likely to be, "I don't believe it." The second reaction: "It won't last." The third: "I liked the old ways better—at least they were something I knew how to deal with."

The result of these reactions is very apt to be one you didn't expect and certainly won't welcome—the child's behavior will worsen for a time rather than improve. He'll test and test and test, trying to get you to revert to the old ways. And, being human, on occasion you will. But if, overall, you're fairly consistent in not falling back into the destructive old patterns, your child may, in time, also begin to change some of his ways. It really happens.

8. How to Stop Having Your Buttons Pushed

GETTING THEIR OWN WAY

At a Families Anonymous meeting in Chicago recently, a distraught mother suddenly burst out, "I keep seeing ways in which I'm overcontrolling, overprotective. But if I'm that much in control, how come my boy still winds up getting his own way so much of the time?"

At first a bit of appreciative laughter, then a babble of voices greeted her. One by one, FA members talked about their own experiences with children who know just how to "push their buttons"—manipulate them to evoke an expression of anger, create a confrontation, or otherwise get what they want. Here, distilled from what these parents had to say, are the major methods that children unconsciously use to manipulate their parents:

Wearing them down. Kathy, a fourteen-year-old, wanted to go to a party given by one of her acquaintances. Her mother felt uneasy about the other girl, suspected that pot was going to be smoked at that party, and told Kathy she couldn't go. For three days straight Kathy, who was used to *not* taking no for an answer, pleaded, threatened, and wept. She knew if she kept it up long enough, her mother would cave in, and so her mother did.

Changing for the better—temporarily. Much of the time Gary was a hostile teenager, surly to his mother and openly contemptuous of his father. Many angry scenes occurred between them. But whenever Gary wanted something special— to borrow the family car on Saturday night, for instance, or to have his full allowance reinstated after it had been cut down as a punishment—he became very nice to his parents. He talked to them politely. He actually smiled at them. He cooperated in doing chores. Very soon he got what he wanted—and then returned to his familiarly hostile ways. This pattern kept repeating itself.

"What they do is methodically soften you up," said Gary's father, a rueful expression on his face, "and it works if you're not careful because you so desperately want to see them doing well, behaving well. You grasp at any straw. You hope maybe this time it's for real. But it never is."

Making promises they don't keep. Phil dropped out of school in the twelfth grade but kept on living at home. He slept his days away, spending his nights smoking marijuana with friends. Whenever his bewildered parents suggested he find a job or maybe even move out and get his own place if he was going to continue leading that kind of life, Phil would fervently promise to straighten out. Yes, he knew the life he led was no good. Yes, he'd find some work pretty soon and get an equivalency high-school diploma. Each time, his parents caved in and let him stay on. More than a year passed.

His mother explained, "We would always think, 'Poor Phil, he so wants to get along in life, and he just can't help it.' But now I think, 'Boy, he really knew how to make us feel sorry for him, how to get around us so we'd go into the poor-Phil bit. We always thought he was so naïve, but he was a lot cleverer than we gave him credit for."

Holding out some bait. David's parents valued education highly; they wanted all their sons and daughters to go to good universities and receive fine educations, and they were prepared to make any sacrifice toward that end. In fact, they'd begun saving for that goal before the first of their four children was even born. When David, the oldest, was seventeen he wanted his parents to buy him a van. They told him no, not only because they didn't feel they wanted to make that big an expenditure but also because his schoolwork was shaky and he'd been cutting some classes.

"Well, he knew how much we wanted him to go to college, and he played that to the hilt," his mother recalled. "He told us he thought he might just drop out of school and get a job so he could save enough money to buy himself that van. But if we got him the van, he said, he'd get the best marks he could and go on to college. Well, we got him the van. And it's not hard to figure out what happened next. He managed to finish high school somehow, but his grades were so poor there was no hope of getting him into any decent college. Now he says he's sorry—and now it's too late."

Saying or doing something they know will enrage their parents. The unconscious aim: to evoke a strong reaction—fury, anxiety, or extreme discomfort—on the parents' part. Thus a girl who knows her parents are quite sensitive about her in relation to sex may hint at having slept around. A child who knows a certain look or mannerism is very upsetting to one or the other parent may use it specifically to get the parent upset. In effect, this child is thinking, "I push the button, see him (her) jump!" So it was with Donna and her father, a man who had near-perfect control in his business dealings but, by his own admission, couldn't handle something his daughter did.

"Donna had a way of being insolent that really made me see red," Donna's father said. "I suppose I fell for that trap the first or second time she did it and got such a violent reaction from me. Anyway, she seemed to have an uncanny way of knowing just how to make me jump with anger. And—I couldn't help noticing—she'd walk away from those heated exchanges with a tiny little smile on her face. Wasn't till much later that I realized the significance—she was *enjoying* those scenes."

Playing off one parent against the other. Susie wanted to have her own telephone credit card. When her mother said, "No way," Susie called her father at his office. She asked him for the same thing—not bothering to mention the fact that her mother had already said no. Father didn't say no—but he was hesitant. So Susie worked on him—"sweet-talked me to death," her father said—until he gave in.

Susie's father readily admitted her ploy couldn't have worked if he and his wife had been seeing eye to eye on how to raise their daughter. But they were having sharp disagreements about that; he thought his wife was much too hard on the girl. That was partly what made him susceptible to her sweet-talk.

Playing on their parents' fears. The equation goes something like this: "If you don't give me what I want, dire things will happen to me—and it will be all your fault!" The threat to hitchhike illustrates this perfectly. "Annette wanted to visit a friend of hers on the West Coast last summer, and we decided that at sixteen she was too young to travel alone like that," the girl's mother related. "So we said no, we wouldn't give her the fare. Annette took it very calmly. She didn't fly off the handle, as she often does when she doesn't get her own way. But a few days later she hit us with it. 'Okay, if that's the way you feel, I'll hitchhike to L.A.," were her exact words. And she repeated them a few times the next few days. Each time she said it, it was like an icy grip on my heart—I could see Annette robbed, raped, maybe even murdered if she hitchhiked. Her father was frightened, too. So we gave in, as she must have known we would, and gave her the fare."

Threats to run away or to commit suicide are extreme forms of manipulation; being extreme, it must be assumed that the boys and girls who use them are very distraught. There's Rosa, who ran away once and now threatens to go again whenever she doesn't get her own way. "And a lot of the time she has me," Rosa's mother admits. "I go into a panic at the thought of her taking off again, being out there somewhere, God knows where. The first time, she was gone three weeks, and when she got back she looked a mess but wouldn't tell us where she'd been. I still have that picture in my mind."

Even more agonized are the parents whose children threaten—or make halfhearted attempts—to commit suicide. Sylvia's mother told the Families Anonymous meeting in Chicago her unhappy story—she'd been "nagging Sylvia something terrible about dressing sloppily, keeping her room filthy, and coming home so late at night. We'd get into these terrible rows. She'd cry and cry. Said she wished she was dead. And a couple of times she actually slashed her wrists. So I'd feel just awful, and think five times about saying anything to her that smacked of discipline, and see her run wild, and say something, and have the whole thing start all over again."

How Manipulation Is Destructive—Three Ways

1. Successful manipulation teaches a child that not being straight—or direct—is the best way to get along in life; that it's wrong, or risky, or self-defeating, to ask for things directly.

2. Manipulation as a way of life actually makes it harder to get along in life; it is very difficult for manipulative children ever to accept no for an answer—they simply keep trying to manipulate that no into a yes, and are in a constant state of tension trying to change things to the way they want them. (And the manipulative child becomes the manipulative adult.)

3. When children manipulate specifically to get their parents angry or anxious—and when their parents do display the intended reaction—the children correctly perceive their parents as being out of control. This then reinforces their own

feelings that it's permissible to lose control; after all, if Mother or Father can do it, why not they?

WHY CHILDREN MANIPULATE

Most, if not all, younger children are somewhat manipulative; it goes with the age. As they grow older, boys and girls generally tend to be more "up front." A ten-year-old will "seduce" his mother for three days trying to get her to change her mind about not letting him go to a Boy Scout jamboree; the typical adolescent who's told she can't go to a dance will be demanding to the point of throwing a tantrum rather than manipulative. When adolescents remain eager to push their parents' buttons, there are reasons why. The main ones follow:

• Boys and girls don't push buttons in a vacuum; family therapists insist that when teenagers use manipulation as a definite and habitual style, they've been seeing a good many manipulative exchanges over the years—mainly at home, between their parents. Says Los Angeles psychotherapist Thomas Waner, "Kids are much more apt to manipulate when their parents are easily manipulative to each other. The kids become pros at it—much better than their parents sometimes—because they've grown up seeing it. Children are like sponges from the time they're born; they just absorb."

• Correctly or not, some manipulative children feel they're not being listened to, not understood—that whenever they ask for something directly the answer is no.

• The children feel overprotected, overcontrolled, and hence powerless. They feel they have to gain some power for themselves; if not directly—if that proves impossible—then indirectly. Manipulating their parents does the trick, lets them feel less weak and dependent, because then they can tell themselves, "I've put something over on the Old Man"—or "Old Lady." It's one of the reasons why some boys and girls push their parents' buttons to elicit anger; after all, the button pusher is the one in control.

How to Tell Whether You're Being Manipulated and What to Do About It if You Are

Sometimes parents don't realize it when their children are being manipulative with them, so the pattern goes on repeating for months, maybe years. It becomes an established way of interaction without any family member's being consciously aware of it. How can you tell whether you're being manipulated? Ask yourself these questions:

Do any of the manipulative patterns described in this chapter seem to hit home—*your* home, that is?

Do you often feel as if you've been had by your child? As if you've been victimized?

Do you often feel irrationally angry with the child—angry without being able to pinpoint the exact source of the anger?

Do you often feel that issues related to this child get out of hand before you can put a stop to things?

Do you often find yourself saying yes when you really meant to say—or stick with—no?

If the answer to any of these questions is clearly in the affirmative, it's safe to assume that some manipulation is going on. And if it is, what then? Can you put a stop to it? Definitely, even if it has been going on for years and years. Many parents who belong to FA have been in exactly this situation, and have worked out ways of bringing the manipulative pattern to a sharp halt. Here are some of the ways they've done it:

· They stop allowing themselves to be needled or drawn into a fight. Herbie, a sassy thirteen-year-old, would ask his mother, innocently enough, "What's for dinner?" She'd tell him, and he'd have a little fit of temper because he never liked the dishes she chose to cook. Mother would then try to assuage him—justifying, explaining why that particular meal was being served. By the time dinner was actually on the table, she was left feeling irritable if not exhausted. This occurred regularly, like the proverbial clockwork. And now? Now, when he starts ranting, she simply lets him go on. She refuses to respond. At first it was hard for her to restrain herself; it took a lot of conscious effort, of willpower. But it became easier each time, and when he saw he couldn't push his mother's buttons any more, Herbie stopped having so many fits.

• Delayed reaction is a simple counterstratagem that some parents, former victims of angry-children-turned-sweet-until-they-get-what-they-want, learn to adopt. They check their pleasure at seeing the newfound sweetness; they don't jump to say yes to their children's request. They're determined not to give an automatic no, either, because then they would still have been jumping at the push of the button. Instead, they practice delaying their reaction; they tell their children they will have to think about the matter and then calmly deliberate the particular issue *on its own merits,* regardless of how cooperative their children are just then or how hostile they've been two days earlier. The parents can then sometimes say yes, sometimes no, and not feel manipulated.

• The principle of delayed reaction has also been adopted successfully by some mothers and fathers who were played off one against the other, as in the case of Susie and the telephone credit card. Each parent tells the child, "I can't give you an answer till I talk it over with your mother"—or "father." They don't make snap decisions, don't say yes or no until they've had a chance to confer together.

• Parents who have been the target of threats—like the fairly common one of "I'll hitchhike"—no longer rise to the bait. And they refrain from lecturing on the dangers of hitchhiking. What they do instead is to place the responsibility where they feel it squarely belongs—on the child who threatens. Thus, one mother of a teenager who threatened to thumb

her way across three states said, "Wow, I wouldn't go hitchhiking if you paid me, I'd be too afraid." Then she outlined exactly
what she was genuinely afraid of. In conclusion this mother
said, "But of course it's your choice, your decision." Most of
the parents who have learned to act this way say that since the
threats lost their power their youngsters stopped threatening—
and in most instances neither did they hitchhike or otherwise
carry out their threats.

·Threats to run away or to commit suicide are unques-
tionably much more difficult for mothers and fathers to handle.
Parents feel caught; they don't want to be doormats for their
youngsters, but don't want to ignore the potential seriousness
of the situation, either. The father of a fourteen-year-old boy
who took off once and then repeatedly threatened to run away
again finally told his son, "I love you and I don't want you to
run. But I simply can't let you have your own way in everything
—wouldn't be good for you, for me, or for the rest of the
family."

Because of their life-and-death quality, suicide threats are
trickiest. Even if used manipulatively and the children involved
really don't mean to kill themselves, those children may finally
convince themselves that suicide is indeed the best way out. Or
pretend to commit suicide—some children nick their wrists or
swallow a few sleeping pills—but then accidentally go too far.
After hearing many suicide threats from their boys or girls,
there are FA parents who finally say, as one mother did, "I
don't want you to do it, but in the end it's your life, your
decision, and I can't save you."

In this instance and in a number of other, similar ones,
the boys and girls involved stopped threatening; nor did they
make any further suicide attempts. But it's an admittedly risky
approach; the child who hears such a remark may interpret it
as coming from an uncaring parent, may see it as further proof
of being unworthy, and may go ahead to "show" the parent
that he or she did indeed mean it.

Runaway and suicide threats should always be seen—and heard—as serious cries for help; that's so whether or not there's a manipulative element to them. If you as a parent are the target for such a threat, your reaction may be one of fear or anger—more likely, a combination of the two. Try instead to focus on the very real fact that this is a child in much pain, under a great deal of stress—for whatever reason, a very needy child.

Counselors suggest: You can't allow yourself to be black-mailed by such threats, for then the child involved simply takes over, and this, too, is an extremely unhealthy situation. Do what you can to ease pressure on the child. Issues like clothes or hair or homework aren't really important when so much distress is being expressed. Keep rules to a minimum (good advice in any case). Make it clear that you love the child very much and don't want to see the threat carried out—but that you can't abdicate your responsibility for involving yourself in certain crucial decisions involving the child and that some-times those decisions may be counter to what she or he wants. Try if at all possible to get competent professional help; the guidance of a professional skilled in the treatment of adoles-cents can be invaluable in situations like these.

As the situation changes, the threats often taper off. Oc-casionally they don't, though, even after the family has had extensive counseling, after the parents have learned to shift their focus from their children to themselves, and after the distressed offspring have been shown steadfastly loving con-cern. What then? Then the parents must learn to accept the fact that they will from time to time hear those threats made, and that a threat may even, one day, turn into a terrible reality; they're powerless to control this and must learn somehow to live with it.

A father named Hugh has learned to live with his daugh-ter Karen's situation. Karen has run away twice and now, at home, periodically, unexpectedly, threatens to kill herself.

She's steadfastly refused therapy. Her parents consulted one psychologist who recommended hospitalization, another who said hospitalization would be the very worst thing in the world for her. She threatened to run from any institution; told them if they tried anything like that, they would never see her again.

Of his daughter, Hugh now says, "We still tread very lightly with Karen. We tread very lightly and hope it won't happen, but we're also learning to accept the fact that some things are out of our control, so it might happen. However, we say—and we believe—that we would not be contributors to its happening, so if it did, we wouldn't be having overwhelming feelings of guilt. In the end it *is* her life and only she has the ultimate say over what happens to it."

9. Why Parents Shouldn't Be Rescuers

Parents know that at least one of their important roles is to protect their children—to keep them out of harm's way, to help them as best they can when they're in need of help, and to rescue them when they're in danger or serious trouble of any kind.

However, parents also know that things aren't that simple. Children can't be protected from all of life's contingencies or hazards, not even if parents or bodyguards were right there to look after them twenty-four hours a day. So parents know they have to strike a balance between protecting their young ones and preparing them to face risks and hazards, to deal with problems, to make appropriate judgments, and to accept and overcome hurt and unhappiness—in effect, preparing them to grow up.

As has been stressed, rebellion is a normal, expected phase in children's adolescent years, especially in early adolescence. But in time most adolescents outgrow the rebellious stage. When, instead, their rebellion becomes more intense and prolonged, the adolescents involved aren't growing up. It's a fact of life that in the history of many if not most seriously rebellious adolescents one can see that they were overprotected as children. Here are a few of the ways it happens:

·An adult still crossed the street with them long after other children of the same age were allowed to cross alone.

· They were carefully watched in the playground to make sure they didn't skin their noses or scrape their knees; if they somehow did, a big fuss was made about it.

·Their parents became very anxious when they first started going to school.

· Their parents very quickly interceded when they got into fights with friends, peers, or teachers.

·Their parents delayed letting them go on sleep-over dates; their friends were allowed to go on them much sooner.

· Their parents were always there to rescue them from the consequences of their own mistakes.

Rebellious adolescents not only cross the street by themselves, they're apt to be more street-wise in certain respects than their parents ever were or will be after a lifetime of living. But many of these youths, in one very significant manner, are still being overprotected: Their anxious, loving mothers and fathers rescue them whenever they get into jams.

Few youngsters of any age are going to rebel or protest when their parents help them get out of jams. But a regular pattern of rescue gives rise to conflicting or otherwise troubling feelings in the rescued youngsters:

"If they keep taking care of me like this I must be pretty helpless."

"Guess they feel I'm not smart enough to figure out my own life."

"Doesn't matter what kinds of scrapes I get into, my folks will get me out of them."

"Since I'm not responsible for my own actions, I won't ever have to pay the price for screwing up."

THE CHILD'S RESPONSIBILITY

To repeat June Toellner's very important statement in Chapter 6: "Each person in a relationship has one hundred percent responsibility for that relationship. Each person, regardless of age, is fully responsible for himself and for what happens to him in the family setting. When there's a breakdown in the family, it doesn't make sense to ask, 'Whose fault is it?' It could be everybody's fault and nobody's fault. That means, when it comes to change, each person has to take responsibility for himself."

If that holds true for you, the parent, it's equally valid for your children. Sooner or later, in the general course of growing up, children are going to have to learn that their behavior, good and bad, brings on consequences, good and bad; that they must own up to and pay for their mistakes just as older people do; that, like everybody else, they have to take responsibility for their actions. The young child learns: Touch a hot stove and you get burned. The older child learns: Steal or deliberately break other people's property and, if you are caught, you get punished. The adolescent learns: Cut classes and you fall behind in your schoolwork; fall behind far enough and you won't graduate. But young rebels don't, or can't, learn such lessons—or learn them well enough—because their well-meaning parents unknowingly deprive them of this essential learning by doing too much for them.

What's too much? Here are some examples:

•They make a practice of writing phony excuses for a child who oversleeps and is often late for school, or for a child who frequently plays hooky.

•They give money to a teenager who's a heavy user of drugs.

•They allow a careless young driver to drive the family car (or they even buy the youngster a car of his or her own).

•They make excuses to neighbors angry because of the antics of the rebellious child.

•They pay off bill collectors for an irresponsible offspring, or for one who's a drug addict.

In one way or another the parents keep trying to cater to, or appease, the rebellious child. Mary's mother used to be like that. It was her nightmare that her daughter became involved with a drug pusher and, at seventeen, moved in with him. Then she became involved in a series of organized thefts. "When she first started seeing the pusher, I thought I could still keep her. I did all the things I could for her—washed and ironed her things, drove her to work. I thought, 'Maybe if I do all these things she'll turn around, be nice, come to her senses.' But I could have stood on my head and it wouldn't have changed things."

Lydia's mother has a similar story to tell: "Lydia was the difficult child in the family and we used to plan all family activities, including vacations, around her. We were hoping Lydia would go with us—and not spoil things if she *was* with us. No matter what it was, we'd always try to please Lydia because she was so negative about everything. But none of it worked."

Consider Jenny's story. Jenny was a quarrelsome girl of fifteen who professed to hate her mother, popped bennies, and hung out (despite her mother's pleadings) with a gang of tough street kids in this socioeconomically mixed Boston neighborhood. She had a falling out with one of the girls; this girl often threatened to beat her up. Whenever the threats really frightened Jenny she called her mother, a single parent who worked as a secretary in a law office, to come and stay with her. Sometimes she did so. Jenny's relationship with the other girls deteriorated and she was finally excluded from the gang. Friendless now, Jenny begged her mother to sell her house and move to a new neighborhood, where the girl could "start fresh." She made innumerable promises to straighten out her life. Though Jenny's mother loved the house and the neighborhood, she finally gave in. Three weeks after moving to another section of town, Jenny found a new circle of friends—again, street kids and school dropouts.

WHY RESCUED CHILDREN AREN'T SAVED

Oftentimes parents become rescuers because, consciously or not, they feel guilty over the fact that *they've* made mistakes, that they haven't been the parents they should have been. "I'll do all these things for my child because I've been deficient in so many other ways" is how the thinking goes. But in reality they can't make up for their own mistakes any more than they can for their children's—certainly not by rescuing. Young persons who run away, become drug addicts or dealers, drop out of school, or otherwise act in ways injurious to themselves and to society may hurt inside—*do* hurt inside—but must also take responsibility for choosing to act as they do. To stress again: Not every child whose parents have made the same mistakes as other parents runs away or becomes an addict or deals in drugs or stops going to school or shows other problem behavior; very many don't.

Psychotherapist June Toellner puts it like this: "Teenagers sometimes turn to their parents and say, 'If you'd been more understanding,' or, 'If you'd only treated me like a person,' or, 'If you hadn't been drunk every weekend,' or, 'If you hadn't been this way or that way—then I wouldn't be the way I am now.' But that's a cop-out. A child can't blame his parents for the rest of his life and absolve himself of responsibility that way. The child is still responsible for the way he acts."

When she talks to the children themselves, Ms. Toellner stresses, she says exactly the same thing: "What you do with your parents' behavior—how you react to your parents—is your own responsibility."

Even more importantly, when young people—for that matter, people of any age—see they can get away with things they shouldn't, there's no incentive for them to change. Having failed to learn that they are indeed responsible for the choices they make, the actions they take, they fail to understand the consequences of their actions. And fail to profit from their mistakes.

Another thing: As already noted, boys and girls who are always saved from the consequences of their behavior do on some level tend to feel pretty helpless. They become (or remain) as self-centered as babies—preoccupied with surviving in a harsh world in which they feel so helpless. This is one reason why parents of very rebellious children can keep giving, appeasing, and rescuing without getting much of any appreciation. Nothing's ever enough when one is feeling that helpless—that inadequate.

Finally, children who aren't allowed to take responsibility for their actions never learn inner controls—never learn to govern or censor their own actions. They remain extremely impulsive as well as self-centered. Lacking these inner controls, what controls there are in their lives have to come from the outside—such as the ever-watchful eyes of their parents, their teachers, the police, the courts, or whatever authority figures are at hand.

All this adds up to a persuasive conclusion: To rescue is to perpetuate the problem; to stop rescuing is to give the child a chance to experience the pain—and ultimately the pleasure —of growing up.

This is admittedly a very hard task to carry out, not only because the rescue pattern is probably well entrenched but also because parents don't want to see their children suffer. In fact, they suffer when their children do—often to the point where they lose their perspective on what will be best for the children in the long run. Yet many parents who have been rescuers for years and years have finally been able to stop the practice, and have ultimately enjoyed the benefits both to themselves and to their children.

To stop rescuing is to start letting go, letting the child mature and become more independent. In FA circles this is called "release with love," and the next two chapters will describe how some mothers and fathers have managed it with their rebellious boys and girls.

10. "Release with Love"

How They Release

Irma, the mother of an eighth-grader named Shirley, hated schoolday mornings. It almost always turned out to be the same unpleasant routine. Irma would awaken Shirley, and Shirley would immediately go back to sleep. After a few minutes Irma would awaken the girl again. The same thing would happen. The third time she was awakened, Shirley snarled rudely at her mother. Irma's own temper flared then, and they would quarrel until Shirley decided to get up. Finally, Irma learned to release her daughter with love—and with an alarm clock. She bought the clock, handed it to Shirley, and told her that from then on she was responsible for waking herself up.

Shirley insisted she'd forget to wind the clock or sleep through the alarm, but Irma held firm. The first two mornings Shirley really did oversleep and was late for school, but Irma refused to write the school a note explaining away the lateness. "It's your responsibility to get yourself up on time," she told Shirley. The third morning—and with few lapses thereafter—Shirley did get herself up on time.

For a father named Tony, release came after his son, Jeff, got into his second automobile accident. Jeff, an eleventh-grader, had been doing poorly in school and, though he steadfastly denied it, his father suspected him of being a fairly heavy user of drugs. Still, when Jeff made a strong pitch about really buckling down in school if he could just have a car of his own, like a lot of the other guys did, his father bought him a nice used car. Three months after he got it, he and some friends were driving around at night when they slipped on the wet pavement and rolled down an incline. Amazingly, nobody was hurt, but the car was pretty badly wrecked. Since Jeff had been doing better in school and the circumstances of the crash were blurry, Tony decided to take another chance. He got Jeff a second car, especially after Jeff promised not only to keep up his grades but to get a part-time job as well.

The boy did get a job, in a supermarket, but his grades started slipping again. Within a couple of months, driving home from a party, he got into another crash. Though there was some suspicion of marijuana having been smoked in the car, again nobody was hurt, and the police didn't make a fuss. But this time, despite Jeff's pleadings, Tony refused to put up the money to have the car repaired or to buy Jeff another one. For nearly a week Jeff sulked about, going neither to school nor to work. On the fifth day, however, he walked the mile to school and that afternoon took a bus to the supermarket where he worked. Since then he's been showing up in both places regularly, Tony reports—and without a car.

Bruce's way of releasing Charley, his son, was a hard one —maybe the hardest thing he ever had to do. Charley became a pothead very soon after he was first introduced to marijuana, when he had just turned seventeen. It didn't take long for him to drop out of school and hang out with his new friends, most of whom were also high-school dropouts. After a few weeks he went back to school, but intermittently. Next he was arrested for possession of marijuana. He was let off on condition that he see a psychiatrist, which he did, briefly. Then he stopped going to school altogether. Finally, at nineteen, he left home to live on his own. He worked as a laborer to support himself, but shortly was arrested a second time for possession of mari-juana. His desperate parents got him the best lawyer they could hire; the lawyer succeeded in getting Charley off on probation. But nearly a year later, Charley was arrested again—this time for selling an ounce of pot to a woman who turned out to be an undercover narcotics detective. Charley ran to his father for help, but this time—and this is what was so hard for Bruce to do—he refused his aid.

Bruce said later, "I'd already taken it upon myself to warn Charley well ahead of time—that if he got into trouble again it was his problem. I told him, 'If you want to go out and do things the way you have, then do whatever you want. But it can no longer involve your mother and me because we can't go through it again. We'll always be your parents, but we won't get you out of jail again. We love you, but we can't spend the rest of our lives—whatever time we have left—suffering and suffering for you."

At the time Bruce related this story, Charley was in jail, serving an eight-month sentence.

Ruth and Martin's release came in the form of their determination to quit worrying about their daughter, Cora, who's seventeen. At sixteen, Cora went through a period of intense sexual activity with a number of boys—then, despite her parents' protestations, settled down to one boy roughly her own age and moved out to live with him. Her parents felt that the boy was dirty and unkempt and that he had values wholly inconsistent with their own. But what bothered them most was that Cora refused to use contraception. Ruth often tried to get her daughter to Planned Parenthood, but Cora steadfastly refused, "I'm not stupid, I'm not going," was her typical reply. The girl Cora's boyfriend lived with before her had been preg-nant twice before they broke up. Cora's answer to that: "So big deal. Anyway, Tim says if I get pregnant we'll get married."

Such attitudes were heartbreaking to Ruth and Martin, who loved their daughter dearly—still do—and worried about her constantly. But in time they learned that, for their own emotional survival, they had to let go. They had to release. And so, eventually, they did. "We sometimes think about it and start worrying, but then we catch ourselves," Ruth says. "And we say—we have to say—that we've tried. There's nothing more we can do about it. It's her problem."

For Karen's parents "release with love" meant the ultimate form of letting go—that is, saying good-bye. They describe their daughter, an asthmatic, as having been a spoiled and overprotected child. They readily acknowledge having sheltered her too much—mostly because she's an only child and has the asthmatic condition—but say her behavior problems really started when both her parents became seriously ill at almost the same time. This happened shortly after she turned seventeen. Her mother had just had a mastectomy. Karen let her schoolwork slide, began smoking cigarettes and marijuana for the first time (terrible for her asthma, but she didn't care), acted nastily to her parents, refused to do chores, and became sexually involved with a high-school dropout her parents termed a "bum." After months of stormy parent-child quarrels, Karen at last told her parents to go to hell and moved in with her boyfriend. She refused to return to school.

Another three months passed—agonizing months for Karen's parents. One day Karen called them and sounded friendly; it became obvious she wanted to reestablish contact. Having learned a few things about such situations by then, however, her parents were very careful in this phone conversation. They didn't show anger. They didn't try to make Karen feel guilty for her behavior (as they had tried to do in the past). Karen's response was to phone them regularly from then on. And one evening, just after saying hello, she made the announcement they'd been longing to hear: "I want to come home."

Happy—but wary, too—the girl's mother and father met her for lunch. Yes, she repeated, she wanted to come home.

"We're very glad to hear that," they said, "but we don't want things to go on as they were before you left. Will you," they asked her bluntly, "be willing to abide by our standards of conduct?"

Karen's answer: "No."

Her father's answer to that was gentle but firm. "We don't have the right to ask you to change the way you live, Karen; we *can't* make you change. But we do have the right to uphold certain standards in our home. So, under the circumstances, it's best if you don't come home. You'll be eighteen soon, so the wisest thing is for you to start thinking about getting a place of your own."

Karen looked stricken. Her mother had to hold herself quite still to keep from saying, "Karen, darling, I don't care what you do, just come home," but she and her husband had agreed that they couldn't again go through the hell they'd gone through with Karen for the last seven or eight months before she left. Karen's father then went on to say, "Honey, we have a right to lead decent lives. Our lives were being absolutely destroyed, and no one, not even you, has a right to do that to us."

COPPING OUT?

So this is what "release with love"—letting go, not being the overprotective parent—means for such mothers and fathers. It means becoming less emotionally involved, being willing to let their children take responsibility for themselves, allowing them to deal with things on their own, *handing them the problems that are properly theirs.*

Those problems may be as relatively trivial as early-morning arguments or as serious as a possible jail term. While generally the mothers and fathers who learn to release do so after repeatedly failing to "reach" their rebellious, hostile, and uncooperative children, they also find the principle working well with their other, less troubled or untroubled children. Irma's alarm-clock solution is a good example. As much as they possibly can, releasing parents let their children do the following:

· Assume responsibility for their own lives.
· Learn from their own mistakes.

This doesn't mean they will never help their children again, will never bail them out when they're in trouble. Whether or not they do depends on the circumstances. It does mean they don't continue in the role of rescuers *as a way of life.* They know their limits now. They make it very clear to their offspring what those limits are. And, insofar as they humanly can, they remain consistent in this.

"We have a right to lead decent lives," Karen's father told his daughter, and this too is what "release with love" is all about. Most often parents in crisis situations begin to let go of their children when they themselves can no longer stand the tension, the intense anxiety they feel, the sorrow for themselves and for their children. They've realized by then that they can't change these children they so desperately want to save, that whatever impetus for change does come will have to emanate from the rebellious young ones themselves. They've come to recognize their own powerlessness; they're no longer possessed of the "arrogance to think we can shape them as we want them to be."

Those words came from Celia, a mother whose daughter ran away from home four times in six months. Celia adds, "As parents we want our children to share our experiences, to learn from our errors, but we're really telling them, 'Don't bother to live, I can tell you about it, I can tell you how to do it.' Well, I'm not doing that any more. They have to go through the perils and the songs of life themselves. They have to—that's what life is all about. Everybody has to take some hard knocks. If our children don't have the freedom to fail, they don't have the freedom to succeed, either."

Upon hearing of the release-with-love approach, some mothers and fathers become resistant. Their immediate response is, "First we created these kids' problems, then we cop out on them." But that's those troublesome guilt feelings taking over again. Parents do not single-handedly create their children's problems. In any event, by the time they're ready for the release approach, mothers and fathers don't feel they're copping out; they've tried everything possible and failed. As Celia puts it, "If you bake a cake and it comes out real terrible, and you go on using that recipe, and it keeps coming out terrible, would you continue year after year to use that same recipe to make a terrible cake? The analogy is—I lectured her and scolded her, I took away her privileges, I tried counseling for her and for me, I tried intervening with the school on her behalf . . . And all of it just seemed to make matters worse. So my choice was to continue baking that terrible cake or be willing to accept that maybe there was a better way."

She and other like-minded parents make it clear that it isn't easy to let go after all those years when they have been so protective, so hanging on. Only when they become convinced there's no other way do they begin to release their children—and then not without anguish, without torturing self-doubts. Psychotherapist Thomas Waner explains, "Part of a person's responsible choice as a parent, in teaching his child to be responsible, may be to allow the child to suffer. That's a very hard thing for most parents to do—to stand by and watch their children suffer. It goes against everything they've been taught as parents."

OUTSIDE RESISTANCE

The world doesn't exactly burst into vigorous applause when parents of extremely rebellious children finally shift responsibility to the children themselves. Relatives often have a hard time understanding just what's going on, why the parents won't be rescuers any longer.

"Jason's grandmother just couldn't get it through her head why I wasn't running down to school any more, pleading with the principal not to expel him," says the mother of a tenth-grader who, for six long months, hardly ever showed up in school more than a couple of times a week. " 'Don't you care if he gets kicked out of school?' his grandmother kept asking. 'Yes, Mother, I care very much.' 'Then why don't you do something about it?' she'd say. 'I am doing something about it, Mother, I'm making Jason face up to his behavior. For months now I've been pleading with Jason, and trotting down to school, and weeping and wailing to keep the principal from dumping him. I've even taken him bodily to school and found out later he'd go in the front door and right out the back door. It hasn't been helping Jason and I've felt like I've been through the wringer. Now Jason knows I'm not going to run interference for him again, and if they expel him, then they expel him.'

"So then Mother wails, 'But then he won't graduate; it's terrible, terrible!' Then I say, as calmly as I can, 'If he doesn't go to school he can't graduate, that's true. And he knows it—and if it's his choice to be truant, he'll have to take the consequences. If at some future time he feels he wants to finish school and get his diploma, then he'll do so—or take an equivalency exam, or something. But it has to be up to him. I can't take him by the hand and lead him to school; I can't chain him to his desk.' That settles it for the moment; the next time I talk to my mother we go through the same thing again."

Neither are school people happy when hitherto concerned —if not hysterical—parents finally decline to get involved.

What happened in the case of Buford, a seventeen-year-old, a chronic truant, is an example. Buford's mother says she used to talk her guts out, trying to persuade the school's administrators to give him yet another chance.

"But then I learned I wasn't helping him at all by getting him out of the hot water he was always into. The next time the school called to ask why Buford wasn't in school, I said, 'You'd better ask Buford.' " The vice-principal was nonplussed when she said that, Buford's mother reports, and said, "You're his mother; don't you know where he is? Don't you care?" She answered only that Buford had been told she was no longer going to involve herself in his school problems, that he'd have to suffer the consequences of his actions. The vice-principal persisted in his theme that Buford's truancy was his mother's responsibility, and she persisted in claiming that Buford would have to be responsible for himself.

"It was so simple when I finally did it," she recalls. "I couldn't believe that that was all I had to do—to turn it back to them. The vice-principal said he'd have to expel Buford. I said, 'You'll have to take it up with him; I don't have any control over that.' To be able to say that and mean it, and not feel guilty . . . Buford was furious when he heard. I told him, '*I* can't go to school so that you can graduate.' Well, he didn't graduate; he was two classes off. Now he says he'll go to night school; we'll see. Education is very important in this family, but when this thing happened with Buford, it wasn't the end of the world."

Buford's mother adds, "A lot of people would say this new attitude—this release-with-love business—is a terrible thing. I used to be very conscious of people's opinions. But I don't care what they say any more. They're not the ones going through the heartaches, the hell. Now I realize that if they haven't been in the situation they can't really say what they would do—or what's the right thing to do."

Parents who have been through it all too many times, and

who ultimately think releasing is the right thing to do, have refused to retrieve their youthful offenders from police stations, have prevailed on courts to keep their children in juvenile halls for brief periods, have arranged for temporary foster-home placement when they felt that all other remedies were exhausted, and have declined to provide bail for sons who were repeat offenders. A mother who now declares herself "reformed" says, "I bailed Tommy out for ten years, and every time I took him out he ended up back in. So there had to be something wrong with the way I was doing things. Finally I got wise; I didn't put him in jail, why should I take him out? So I stopped—and now he's fine, he's straightened himself out."

But, like many schools, the police and the courts also often look askance at parents who finally shift the responsibility for a problem to a child whose problem it is. A San Diego couple, Steve and Beth, are just two of many parents whose vivid experiences bear this out. They've had serious difficulties with both their older and younger sons—but, once they began to attend FA meetings, they stopped dealing with things in the old ways. The latest example occurred when their eleven-year-old boy, Ron, was detained for shoplifting. Beth refused to go down to the hardware store whose manager had called to inform her that Ron had tried to steal some tools. Steve, too, was called; he also refused to pick up his son. "Then we'll have to call the police," the manager said. "Then that's what you'll have to do," Steve said.

Eventually two policemen brought Ron home. They wanted to release him in Beth's custody, but she said no. She explained that Ron had been in trouble before for shoplifting, and had been warned that next time he did it he would be on his own. One of the police officers said, "Then we'll have to take him down to juvenile hall. You don't want him to go there; it's a rough place." When she remained adamant, they tried playing on her emotions in a differently offensive way. Looking around the sprawling house, one of the officers said, "When they see what a nice place you live in, they'll send you a whopping bill for keeping the boy in juvenile hall." Beth still wouldn't budge. At that moment Ron became sassy to the policemen, so they handcuffed him and put him in the police car. One of the officers threw over his shoulder, "At juvenile hall he can get beaten up, raped . . ."

"That's when I nearly gave in," Beth remembers. "I was in such torment. In total shock. Yes, I love my son. I wanted to grab him and hold him and hug him and tell him how much I love him. But I remembered all the other times he stole, and just forced myself to keep quiet. All that shoplifting—what would be next, real burglaries? I had to keep quiet. It was a question of what was best for Ron."

Late that evening the police officers returned—a sergeant accompanying them—bringing Ron home. At first his parents started to protest—to insist upon juvenile hall for him. "But then we saw this look in Ron's eyes; it was something that hadn't been there before," Beth says. "Fear, I guess. For the first time he knew we meant business. He hasn't stolen since."

This family's story ends with a strange twist. "We learned later on that he couldn't have been taken to juvenile hall anyway, not under California law, because he was under twelve," Steve says. "The cops play with your heads."

RELEASE AND RULES

You stop trying to change your children's destructive behavior? You release them to go on their merry—or, more likely, not so merry—ways? Upon hearing such approaches suggested, some parents' imagination takes off over the horizon as they immediately envision a suspension of all discipline and structure—envision their rebellious offspring as becoming even more rebellious, running ever wilder. Maybe it's the prospect of no longer controlling their children by the old methods—

of somehow thinking that the world will go haywire if they don't keep control—that sparks such fears.

The truth is to the contrary. It finally dawns on hitherto overcontrolling and overprotective parents, once they let go: Why should they be so hung up on their children's clothes and hair, the condition of their rooms, and other such issues— issues more properly left with the children, especially as they grow older? And then there's schoolwork. These parents at last realize that they can be after their boys and girls from morning till night, urging them to study, to do their homework, to take school seriously, but if the boys and girls aren't motivated on their own to learn, the only predictable result will be endless hassles. The parents come to understand from long and painful experience that the more pressure they put on, the more those particular children will resist.

"We fought constantly about homework," says a father who claims to have had just that long and painful experience hassling with his kids. "And Mitchell would do it sometimes, just because I pushed so hard, but hate me for it. But when I learned my lesson and backed off, telling him, 'Listen, I can't get your high-school diploma for you; it's going to have to be your responsibility from now on,' it wasn't long before he started poring over those textbooks on his own."

The gist of it is that these parents who have had such frustrating if not horrendous problems with the imposition of rules and expectations whittle these down to a very, very few —to the bare minimum necessary for the proper functioning of that little society known as family. And finally they try, if at all possible, not to impose their rules. They try to draw the children themselves in for a mutual exchange, a discussion— a "negotiation," as the therapists like to say—on what's fair and acceptable to all. Of course, negotiation is easier proposed than carried out. Often neither parents nor children have developed the skills for such a give-and-take. Often there's too much anger—on the part of both parents and children—to allow for it. That's all the more reason to whittle down the rules to as few as possible.

When parents are at this point, the issues they try to negotiate—come to some kind of agreement on with their children are, most commonly:

• Household chores.

• Showing up for dinner (getting the child's agreement to call in if there's a delay).

• Curfew time (and calling in if it can't be met).

• Sex (whether or not an opposite-sex friend may spend the night).

• Drugs (whether or not they may be used at home).

• Friends (only with regard to those of the child's friends who are destructive or disruptive when they come to visit).

Of course, rules aren't negotiated in a vacuum. The child's age is a factor. The parents' level of toleration is a factor. In other words, what can you live with? What can't you live with? It does no good at all to do away with all those rules and regulations and then find there are things going on that drive you up the wall. It's your home as well as your child's, and if things are happening that make you feel acutely uncomfortable, you'll inevitably take it out on your child in some indirect way or other. So these issues take some thought, some feeling for what's best for everyone concerned.

Sex is an example. Many parents flatly refuse to allow their daughters' boyfriends to sleep over; some others feel it's okay or, at the very least, that they can live with it. Another example is drugs. The children may say, "Everybody I know smokes pot." A great many parents say no, we're dead set against it; no drugs of any kind, ever, in the house. (They've learned, by then, that they can give antipot lectures until they're breathless, but that they can do nothing about their children smoking the stuff on the outside.) Other parents—a relative minority, to be sure—do prefer to allow their children to smoke at home, even if they're against pot in principle; they think it best to defuse the issue, make it less of a conflict area between themselves and their offspring. A still smaller number of parents occasionally light up with their children; some such parents have been antipot in the past but have become more tolerant as time goes on.

(While mental health professionals who work with youths heavily into marijuana don't necessarily advocate that you sit down and smoke with your children—many are dead set against it—they do say that the less attention you pay to the child's pot smoking, the less need the child has to rebel around this issue. He or she may not stop smoking altogether—probably won't—but is very apt to cut down on the heavy, rebellious use of the drug.)

George and Myra and their daughter, Annie (introduced in Chapter 1), are a good illustration of how one family, after a period of turmoil, finally—if precariously—resolved the issue of rules and regulations. Annie was chronically truant, shoplifted, committed acts of vandalism, was a heavy smoker of marijuana, and ran away from home the morning she was to attend a new school, a parochial school. When found, she was living in a commune in a poor section of town.

Annie came home as sullen and angry as she had left— and the only reason she agreed to come back at all was that her parents threatened to have the other commune dwellers arrested if she didn't. (Today, they say, they wouldn't apply such pressure). But they realized things couldn't go on as they had been before she left. So they gave her a choice. She could live at home, but would have to abide by some rules they would mutually work out. Or she could live with a relative. "The one thing we won't allow again is to have you run away and bum around," they told the fifteen-year-old girl. "If you do, we'll have to go to the police and the courts."

Annie's parents were hoping she'd choose to live with them and obey their rules, but she opted for an aunt who lived some miles away and whose only stipulation was that she attend school every day. She promised faithfully not to be truant; soon, though, she broke the promise. "You blew it; you'll have to go home," the aunt told Annie.

Once she was home again, the girl and her parents had a family conference. She presented them with a list of complaints about their rigidities and unfair expectations—about their tendency to force her to be as they thought best, the girl of their dreams, rather than accepting her more as the girl she actually was. Her parents thought this fair and reasonable. In turn, they presented her with their "minimum requirements," as they termed them. Both sides gave in on some things. For instance, Myra had had an ironclad rule that Annie wasn't to date until she was at least sixteen and a half; she let down on that one. She gave in on cigarette smoking, something that had also been a no-no. Annie would have to attend school regularly —but, at her suggestion, could play hooky twice a month. Both parents were adamant about marijuana, however; if she smoked pot and got arrested her parents wouldn't help her. She would also be responsible if she got into other kinds of trouble.

A test of sorts came soon after Annie used her mother's car without permission and got a ticket. In traffic court both Annie and her mother faced the judge. Myra told the judge that it was her daughter who had broken the law; therefore she didn't feel it to be her responsibility to pay the fine. The judge thought that that was refreshingly fair; he fined Annie fifty dollars, and when the teenager said she was broke, he gave her a month to come up with the money. So what happened? Annie found herself a job, earned the money, and paid the fine.

George and Myra were careful not to show anger or to apply pressure around this incident. They were wonderfully matter-of-fact about the whole thing. That continues to be their attitude. They tell Annie now that her life is largely her own responsibility "because we trust you, we think you're a worthwhile person." They know that Annie—a very bright and stunningly pretty girl—will probably never be the kind of person they want her to be. But they're grateful that she's trying and that her life is quieter now than it has been for years.

"Annie could be president of the student body or the homecoming queen," her mother says, "so when she starts to do well we have to be very careful because then we sort of start hoping for more, and that would be a pressure on her. And we promised not to pressure. So we have to be very careful and keep life at a daily level—live one day at a time and be grateful that we got through it as well as we did."

11. Release and Good-bye

So far, this is what "release with love" means to the parents who practice it:

•No more rescuing.

•Accepting the children as responsible human beings—responsible in large measure for their lives and for correcting the mistakes they make in life.

•Becoming more detached emotionally in relation to the disturbing, destructive behavior that goes on.

•Expecting adherence to mutually worked-out standards of conduct.

What happens, though, if the children involved continue to lead chaotic lives or, at the very least, break the few rules or understandings that remain? For some FA parents, then, "release with love" becomes release in its ultimate, most controversial form. "If you can't live in a reasonably decent way at home," they tell their children in effect, "then you can no longer live at home."

So it was with Roger, whose sad story was described in Chapter 5—Roger, who enlisted in the Navy to please his father, hated Navy life, used drugs as an escape, went AWOL, got a less than honorable discharge, then alternated between

118

living at home and on the streets. At last, after two years of turmoil, the family had to move for business reasons to a town some fifty miles away. Having been in an FA program for several months by then, Sheila and Pete, his parents, realized it was futile to take Roger with them; he'd simply continue leading his nightmarish life—and making their life nightmarish—in the new place. So they told him that, since he wasn't willing to change his ways, he could no longer live with them. He would have to be on his own.

Roger was visibly shocked by the decision but pretended to shrug it off. He left quietly. A few days later he suddenly reappeared, very high, very mean. Pete was at work, Sheila alone. Roger swore darkly, using the foulest of language in front of his mother. He ranted and raved. He threatened to kill a man he knew. Later he admitted that he'd hoped his mother would change her mind about excluding him from her new home—would rescue him if he seemed badly in need of help, as she'd so often done before. But she quietly told him, "No matter what you feel you have to do, you have to do it. You have to suffer the consequences and pay the penalties, but I can't live your life and I can't climb the walls any more. I'm just going to have to hand you back your life and say, 'Live it.' "

Roger stormed away. His scared but determined mother wondered if she'd ever see him again. Three days later there he was on her doorstep, sober, a clear look of admiration on his face. "You are a far-out lady," he said.

A miracle of transformation? No. A turning point of sorts? Definitely. He did not move in with his parents. But, for the first time, he agreed to enter a drug rehabilitation program. Slowly, Roger conquered his drug addiction, but dropped out of the program before it was fully successful. His shaky sense of self-worth led him to a new crutch—alcohol. Now in his mid-twenties, Roger has a drinking problem. However, he also has a steady job and a nice girl friend.

"And that," says his mother, "is something."

A set of parents named Don and Bernice also had a release-with-love confrontation with their son. Beginning with the tenth grade, Artie started cutting classes, then cutting school, smoking pot, popping pills, and hanging out on the streets—a familiar scenario with respect to very rebellious adolescents. He was arrested, once for possession of drugs, once for loitering, once for passing a bad check. Somehow he managed to finish high school, just barely, dropped out of a local junior college a couple of months after starting, then slept his days away and spent nights doing, his parents say, who-knows-what with friends.

For his parents the torment of living and trying to cope with him seemed unending. In fact, the scenario played on and on for five years, until Artie was twenty. "I still don't know how we could have taken it so long," Don now says, "but somehow you look around and years of your life are gone, gone in smoke and suffering."

Don still remembers the talk he had with Artie when he and Bernice finally decided they'd had enough. This is how he describes it: "I told him I wanted to apologize for all the mistakes I'd made in rearing him. I told him I realized that when he was a youngster I didn't give him the chance to mature, to grow and learn by making his mistakes. He said, 'Yes, that's right, you kept the reins on me; you were too strict.' And I said, 'Artie, I'm still making those mistakes.' He said, 'What do you mean?' And I said, 'I'm depriving you of the ultimate chance, the chance to be on your own.' And he said again, 'What do you mean?' So I said, 'Well, you know, by insisting that you stay here with us, your mother and I are depriving you of the opportunity to learn to be on your own. So we're going to release you from your obligation, we're going to let you move out.' "

Don still smiles, recollecting the scene. "Artie hadn't asked to move out. On the contrary, I think he'd thought he could just vegetate and mooch off us as long as he liked. I don't blame him for that; by not doing anything we led him to think he could. Well, his jaw fell open, but he just looked at me. I said, 'This is February twenty-fourth. July fourth is Independence Day—do you think you could be independent of your parents by July fourth?' Well, by the first of April he'd gotten himself a job and found a house, and he and three other boys rented it. He's doing great now—working regularly and getting raises. He's stopped taking Quaaludes and just smokes a little pot now and then. It was ironic, you know? We'd tried putting him into all kinds of passage and self-help groups and with psychiatrists, and all it got us was that he was all the more determined to show us he was going to do what he wanted. But as soon as we made him responsible for himself, he started doing what we wanted."

And then there are two Minneapolis parents who describe themselves as having been masters at idle threats. For years they had made such threats against their older son, Carl, who was heavily into pot and pills. Things were quiet for a bit after Carl left home at seventeen. Then, when their younger son, Arnold, started smoking pot at fourteen his parents resolved not to make the same mistake with him.

"We hate pot, we don't want it in the house," they told him. "If you must smoke, do it elsewhere. If we catch you smoking here you'll be asked to leave home." Predictably, Arnold was caught smoking at home, once with his friends, once alone. His parents didn't want to toss him out, they say; at the same time, they couldn't face years of uproar and anguish with him as they had with their older son. So when they saw "evidence" for a third time—a marijuana "roach" in his room—they asked Arnold to leave.

"In the end," his mother says, "we understood that we not only couldn't accept his pot smoking, we didn't have to accept it."

When Arnold heard that he was to leave, he shrugged in his typically sullen way, stuffed a few items of clothing into a sleeping bag, and went.

"We didn't know where he was going but we were pretty sure one of his friends would put him up," Arnold's father recalls; his mother adds, "We were scared but somehow feeling good, too. It was as though a problem was no longer controlling us—we were controlling it." The feeling might have left her, she admits, if Arnold had stayed away for a long time. But a few days later, when she returned from a shopping trip, she found him at home.

"You're welcome to stay," his mother told him. "But you know the rules about drugs. Okay?"

For a long time Arnold said nothing. Then, "Well, I guess so."

Six months have gone by, his parents say, and Arnold still hasn't been smoking pot, at least in the house.

REASONS AND RISKS

To outsiders the fact that mothers and fathers—respectable, law-abiding, seemingly stable mothers and fathers—can calmly ask their children to leave home may seem cruel and pitiless. Those who have done it say, "You haven't gone through all the years of suffering, the disruption one rebellious child causes the rest of the family. You haven't tried and tried to reach the child, to change things, and failed." And they say, "We're expressing our faith in these children—our faith that in the end they will learn to manage their lives constructively."

Parents who tell their children to leave—and sometimes even go so far as to change the outside door locks if their offspring flatly refuse to move out—stress that they've used this measure only as a last resort. They're not really causing their children to go—it's the children themselves, by refusing to alter their life-styles in any way, who are actually making this choice. Nor have these parents tossed their children out in a moment of anger; they've given them plenty of warning that what's going on is too disturbing to the rest of the family—to the marital relationship and to the other children. Anyway, they stress, they haven't broken all connections; most of the time there is contact between the parents and their departed children—if not right away, then after a bit. They visit; they talk on the phone. And in many cases the young people are welcomed back if and when they want to lead more regular, more constructive lives.

"Release with love," it's called, but many of the releasing parents admit that initially precious little love is apparent between themselves and the children being released.

"When we asked him to leave, it wasn't with love—I couldn't stand the sight of him,"² is the forthright recollection from the mother of a drug-happy son often in trouble for stealing. "I told him he could live with his father in Florida, but he chose not to, and that was up to him. *I* didn't want him around any more. But I've stopped being the shaking, trembling mess I was because of what was going on with him. Now we can talk again; now I can really say it's release with love."

And this from a father who finally asked his drug-involved daughter to leave home: "First you've got to have a chance to catch up on your sleep, to get yourself together. Then, when it's peaceful in your life for a bit, the anger dissipates. So first it's release, then with love."

Many of the parents in this category insist: Only when these rebellious children are on their own do they have a chance of stopping their destructive acts; only then, too, is it possible for the ugly parent-child rifts to heal. Among FA parents whose rebellious children have gone, many heartening stories make the rounds—stories of formerly unkempt children who, on their own now, make a neat and clean appearance; of children whose rooms at home were pigpens, now keeping their

own apartments whistle-clean; of children who insisted on laz-
ing away the days now getting equivalency high-school di-
plomas and working steadily; of former drug addicts now drug
free or merely smoking pot occasionally.

Of course, there are risks, too—to the children who have
to make their way in the outside world and to the parents.
There's the obvious risk that these boys and girls will not make
it on their own, but will sink ever deeper into drugs or other
self-destructive patterns and end up trying to survive on the
brutalizing streets.

Age is an important factor. It's far easier, of course, to ask
rebellious children in their late teens or their twenties to leave
home than it is to expel younger, more vulnerable ones. Understandably, even in dedicated FA circles, relatively few parents
would do as Arnold's parents did, telling a child only fourteen
years old to leave, regardless of how chaotic the home circumstances are. In his case, it worked, but it's risky.

In the case of minors there's also the risk—to the parents
—that they can be charged with abandonment. When parents
are driven to such an extreme, however, the risk doesn't seem
very important. As one mother who finally showed the door to
her violence-prone sixteen-year-old son bluntly says, "What
does being legally responsible for a child mean if the reality is
that I can't handle that child?"

Mental health professionals have mixed reactions to this
extreme form of letting go. Few would quarrel with the concept that not every set of parents and their adolescent child are
meant to live together, that in some cases it's best for them to
separate. As Dr. Leonard Siegel of New York City, a child
psychiatrist who sometimes helps adolescents and their parents
negotiate an amicable separation, observes, "Just as husbands
and wives sometimes have to say, 'We're bad for each other,'
so do parents and teenagers sometimes have to say it."

He and other experts agree that some adolescents need to
be on their own, need to experience life on their terms, to

assume responsibility for their own welfare and learn what it means to be self-supporting and independent. In this context it may be healthiest all around, they say, for highly rebellious children in their late teens or their twenties to leave the homes in which they've acted out their rebellion.

And younger adolescents? That's a far more controversial question. Many if not most professionals disapprove of younger children's being asked to leave home, especially if the children have nowhere specific to go. Disturbed, distressed children have the hardest time making it on their own, they say, and all the more so if they're fairly young. (Of course, even the younger ones may have been acting out their rebellion in ways that make them fairly street-wise.) Look for alternatives, the professionals say. There may be relatives or friends of the family who will agree to have the child live with them (occasionally two sets of parents exchange children; each child does better with parents not his or her own). Or the parents can petition family court to have the child declared a ward of the court and placed in a foster setting. In more serious cases, the rebellion may be so intense and destructive that intensive therapy or maybe even hospitalization is needed.

Alternatives to simply expelling a child are certainly to be preferred; unfortunately they're often not available or don't work out. Frequently no relative or friend wants to undertake the responsibility, or the child is so angry with adults generally that this solution isn't feasible. Nor, when children don't want to cooperate, do court-imposed solutions usually work out well; many children run from foster settings. Some parents are against foster care on principle; they're convinced that only when implacably rebellious children have to rely solely on their own resources is there any real hope for a change. Then too, in many areas adequate foster care—in the form of foster parents or group homes—is very limited; placement may not be possible for months. As for treatment, in many instances this approach has already been tried without success.

What, then, is the best course for families whose lives are constantly in turmoil because of the behavior of a fourteen-, fifteen-, or sixteen-year-old? The decision is a painful one each family must individually make. Some prefer to wait it out, no matter how much the suffering, until the child is older. Meanwhile, the parents will continue to work, hard at changing themselves and at creating the emotional detachment that makes the situation bearable. And some, however reluctantly, find that they're caught in intolerable circumstances; that it will be better to have the child leave than to have the whole family go down the drain.

Whatever the age of the child who's asked to go, the parents can nurture the legitimate hope that, in time, in a different way, they and the child in question will reunite. It really does happen. It happens because temperaments that chafed badly against each other when in such close proximity no longer chafe, because the children do shape their own lives and come to feel better about themselves, because time really does frequently soothe even the angriest feelings, because— again the work of time—the children at last realize that no matter what mistakes their parents made, they suffered with them, tried to reach them and help them, and offered them therapy, drug rehabilitation programs, and everything else they could think of. They did their best.

So it was in the case of Karen and her parents (first introduced in Chapter 10)—Karen, the asthmatic girl, who moved in with her boyfriend, who eventually wanted to come home but still refused to live by any other standards than her own, and who was then told she would have to find her own place to live because her parents had "a right to lead decent lives."

Karen did find herself a job and move away from her boyfriend. Her parents say she has become much more content with herself and her life. They've wished she would finish high school, but she didn't—and they haven't pushed. That may be one reason why the family has become much closer and happier.

"In letting her go," Karen's mother softly says, "we've gotten her back."

12. The Other Children in the Family

How They React

To greater or lesser degree, the other children in the family are always affected by a sibling's rebellious behavior, whether or not that rebellion is extreme.

In the Manning family, where rebellion was minimal, this is how things went: The oldest child passed through a mildly rebellious stage—if it could even be called that—at fourteen. He sassed his parents a bit, trooped through a department store with a group of friends one day, giving off war whoops, played hooky from school on a few occasions, and forged his mother's name to excuses until he got caught at it. His parents made it clear they disapproved of his actions; occasionally they punished him. But it was all handled in a low-key kind of way, since low-key is how the Manning parents are. Mainly they just tried to be explicit about the kind of behavior they expected from him, no nonsense about it.

When his younger sister became a teenager, she hardly rebelled at all. A bit of sassiness, some tantrums, staying out later in the evenings than she should have—such protests summed up her rebellious stage; there was nothing serious. She, too, knew what her firm but loving parents expected of her, what kind of conduct they consistently wanted her to maintain. The third child was a handful at thirteen and fourteen, though—what with her fiery, independent nature, her peppery little self. The Mannings wisely perceived that she needed more leeway than the other two children—and, within reason, gave it to her. So, like the others, she rebelled modestly, mostly around curfew times and boys, disobeying her parents sometimes, arguing with them a lot, often exhausting them—but still, her passage through early and middle adolescence was fairly uneventful.

In the Richards family, things were bumpier: As each of Mrs. Richards's six children reached their middle teens (Mr. Richards having long before deserted the family), that child ran away. What was going on in the family to cause this phenomenon? Mrs. Richards, who worked long, hard hours in a department store, insisted that the oldest of her children each in turn take care of all the younger ones. For a while each of the oldest did just that, but in time each reacted in the same negative way. They resented the responsibility, resented being tied down and deprived of the fun and play normal to their age. Feeling burdened and unfairly used, they ran. It's safe to assume that as each adolescent ran, that child pointed the way for the next one on the ladder.

In the Holden family, rebellion came to dominate: At fifteen and beyond, the Holdens' son, their second child, followed the pattern of escalating rebellion that does so much to rend the fabric of family life. He began with small rebellions, in response to which his parents kept demanding to know why he couldn't be "good" like his sister, the older child. Then, with tremendous hostility, he went on to truancy, drugs, and disappearances, all of which continued for more than a year. His sister, who loved him deeply, was shattered by his behavior, which rather than making her rebel in turn threw her otherwise off balance. She grieved for him, wept for him, and became so tense and upset that she couldn't concentrate on her job in the local library and was nearly fired. In the end, during the height of the turmoil, she took an extended leave of absence.

"I don't understand this younger generation," she kept saying, though she was only three years older than her brother.

WHY THEY'RE AFFECTED

Regardless of age, all the children in a family become acute observers of how their brothers or sisters are treated by their parents in contrast to themselves. And they all observe in great detail how their siblings behave and react. In the Manning family, for instance, it was clear to the younger ones that the older child was treated with respect and consideration even when engaging in a bit of adolescent misbehavior. By contrast, Mrs. Holden was often on top of her son, judging his behavior against her daughter's even though their temperaments were quite dissimilar. "I could always trust her," she says. "Even as a child she was quite mature for her age—not like her brother at all."

Then, too, older children tend to act as models for the younger ones. This was strikingly borne out by the Richards children. They saw what their mother would expect of them as they grew to be the oldest of the brood. They saw how unhappy their oldest brothers or sisters were in the role of surrogate or quasi parent. They saw what their siblings did about it eventually—so, when their turn came, they also did it —split.

When one child in the family engages in a pattern of self-destructive behavior, it creates a welter of difficult-to-handle emotions for that child's brothers and sisters. There may be a rush of fear, anger, bewilderment, and unhappiness— sometimes even envy.

The rebellious child is so much the center of the parents' world and takes up so much of their emotional energy that the other children are ignored. "I was so blind, so focused in on this one older daughter that I wasn't even aware that I had another daughter or husband," is the way one mother of a drug-addicted child put it. "I was so in tune with all these bad things that were going on that I literally ate, slept, and talked around that older child." It's to be expected that the other children, the children who are ignored and/or taken for granted, will resent it. Sometimes bitterly.

What They Feel

Many parents are reluctant to discuss the highly rebellious child with that child's brothers and sisters, especially the younger children. The rationale: "These other kids are still so young. The less they know about the awful things that are going on, the happier they'll be."

According to professionals who work with troubled families, just the opposite holds true. The less the other children know, regardless of age, the more upset they're apt to become. Children—young children, up to seven or eight particularly—lead very active fantasy lives. At times these fantasies they spin out so easily do run away with them. When they feel jealous or angry or competitive with someone—be that someone mother, father, brother, or sister—they sometimes wish that that person would sicken, or disappear, or even die. If, subsequently, something bad really happens to that person, they hold themselves responsible because of the fantasies they've had. They feel as much guilt as if they'd actually caused the tragic event.

What they need, therefore, is not less talk but more talk. They need to have their fantasies corrected. They need to have it made clear to them that they're not responsible, that they had nothing to do with the rebel's disturbing acts.

Then there is another way in which brothers and sisters of the rebel, whether younger or older, sometimes feel threat-

ened. Apprehensively they wonder: "Can this happen to me?
Will I ever act this crazy? Do I have that kind of craziness in
me?"

How the rebel's siblings will react depends in part on how
well they all get along. If the relationship is mostly a good,
strong, positive one, the siblings are much more likely to be
upset than they would otherwise be. When such closeness
exists, perhaps, say, between a suddenly rebellious son and
other siblings, the siblings also find it quite hard to understand
when parents finally seem to be abandoning the boy, leaving
him to work out his own problems, refusing to bail him out of
jail, or asking him to pack up and go. Their reaction is likely
to be one of utter dismay. In part this dismay stems from
sympathy for the troubled sibling, in part from another fear:
"Will I be abandoned, too, if I get into trouble?"

On the other hand, if this same boy has been picking on
his siblings, has been mean and hurtful to them, they may be
glad he's in trouble. They may even ask their parents to kick
him out.

Siblings may react with curiosity ("What's he up to
now?"), with envy ("Boy, he sure gets away with a lot"), and
with resentment ("Why's he getting all the attention?") to the
rebel's antics. Caseworkers at the Family Service of Los Angeles say it's not unusual for younger brothers or sisters to begin
misbehaving when they feel themselves ignored by their parents. Here's the logic that unfolds:

The well-behaved child thinks, "My brother (or sister)
does all kinds of things that cause big problems."

And thinks, "The more problems he (she) causes, the
more our parents notice him (her)."

And thinks, "I don't cause any problems and I don't get
any notice."

And thinks, "I'll start acting up—then they'll pay attention to me, too."

How to Help the Other Children

When a rebellious child is creating havoc at home, there are a number of things that parents can do to minimize the tension for the other children. Counselors suggest:

• Don't pretend that nothing is going on in hopes that if you don't bring up the touchy subject the other children won't wonder or worry. As already noted, they *will* do so. They can see it plainly when you go around with a distracted or distressed look on your face. They can hear it plainly when you're arguing hotly with the rebel, or trying to straighten things out over the phone. Avoid saying to the other children, "Don't worry, nothing's going to happen." Such well-meant but unrealistic reassurance will only make them all the more apprehensive.

• If the other children don't bring up the problem on their own, it doesn't mean they're not thinking about it; it means they're afraid to ask. It may be that they have horrendous fantasies about having caused the problem. Therefore, take the initiative. Talk to the children in an open, invitational way. Give them a chance to ask questions and express their fears. Try to get them to talk about their feelings. How do they see the situation? Do they give any hint of blaming themselves for what's happening? If they do, if their view of things is distorted, be sure to make it clear to them that Johnny or Jane's troubling acts in no way have anything to do with them.

• Avoid blaming the rebellious child, tearing the rebel down. If you do a hatchet job on that child, you create a conflict of loyalties in the other children. They may be unhappy about the events that are transpiring. They may have a lot of sympathy for what you're going through. But that doesn't mean they necessarily want to take sides against their brother or sister. If they feel they're forced to, they'll end up feeling all the more anxious and guilty. Express your disapproval of the disturbing, destructive behavior without tearing down the person. This is what one mother said in such circumstances: "We as a family aren't condemning your brother. We don't like the things that are going on, but we care about him, love him, and we're all going to try to pull together through this crisis."

• If one of the rebellious child's brothers or sisters initiates an attack on the rebel, don't join in. Here's another chance for you to make it clear that, while the rebel's behavior distresses you greatly, the rebel as a person is still your loved child.

• If you're asked to send the rebel away, and you're not prepared to take that step, make it clear. But try also to respond to whatever feelings of anxiety and anger prompted the request in the first place. When a rebellious teenager's younger sister, tired of being picked on by him, told their mother to get rid of him, the parent replied, "I understand how you feel and why you want your brother to go away. But sending him away might not be the best thing for him. I love him as I love you, and I do want to see if there's anything else we can do to help him. But I promise to protect you as much as I can when he's mean to you."

• If there's an especially stable and mature child in the family, you may want to lean on that one, turn to that child for solace and support in the stress of all the disturbing events. But, if you can possibly help it, don't—at least not on a regular basis. Here again, divided loyalty becomes an issue. Then, too, most children come to feel very burdened when their parents keep talking to them about the outrageous conduct of one of their siblings. Some can cut off the talk when it gets to be too much. "I've had it, Mother—not another word about Ricky," is what one girl in her late teens finally said after her mother had engaged her in the two hundredth talk about Ricky's terrible acts. But some children aren't able to set limits like that one; they just suffer in silence—in time either withdrawing or showing their own pent-up anger in some unfortunate way.

• Avoid, too, turning one of the other children into an informer. When a teenager named Paula first started acting strangely, cutting school and hanging out with a bunch of "parkies," her parents pumped her older brother for information about the things she did. They wanted to know if she smoked marijuana, if she seemed to be sexually promiscuous, and the like. At first the boy dutifully answered their questions, but he quickly became very uncomfortable. He started avoiding his parents. In time, fortunately, his parents realized he was dodging their questions and talked to him about it. He told them he loved them and loved his sister. He knew their questions were prompted by their concern for her well-being, and he wanted to help them by telling them what he knew about Paula's activities. But at the same time he felt he was betraying her by informing on her behind her back. His is a typical reaction.

•Even if things are extremely trying in connection with the rebellious child, do your best not to ignore the other children—or for that matter, any of the other members of the family. Make every effort to continue family life as normally as possible. The less the other children's lives are changed or disrupted by the rebel's behavior, the safer they will feel, and the fewer problems they'll evidence because of that behavior.

13. How to Deal with the Peer Group

ADOLESCENT INFLUENCES—BAD AND OTHERWISE

"If Larry weren't running around with that bunch of rough kids he wouldn't be so wild."

"Doris was quiet and sweet, a really cooperative child, until she became friends with Tamara and a member of Tamara's crowd. Now she's impossibly rude and hostile to us —and, yes, I blame it on that crowd, on that influence."

"Dan knew nothing about drugs—marijuana or uppers or downers or any of them—till he latched on to that gang of hippie dropouts that's always hanging around the shopping mall."

When parents discern changes in their children's behavior—objectionable changes, it usually turns out—they often externalize. That is, they often attribute these changes to outside influences, most frequently to undesirable members of their children's peer groups. In fact, loads of books and magazine articles have dealt with the supposedly awesome power of the adolescent peer group.

Why does the peer group play such a powerful role in adolescent life? It's with their peers that adolescents share the whole crazy, scary, exciting process of growing older, growing up, in a way they can't with adults. After all, adults aren't going through that unique experience just then—and, for the most part, have forgotten how lunatic a time it sometimes was. It's with peers that most adolescents feel most comfortable in talking about the really sensitive things that are happening to them—to their bodies, for instance, in their emerging adult sexuality. It's the peer group that gives them a kind of temporary psychological anchor or support as they engage in the crucial business of separating from their parents.

An article in the professional journal *Adolescence* does a neat job of summing it all up: "It is there, in close relationship with their own age-mates, that they seek acceptance and approval, find security, attempt to exert power and, perhaps most important, test out in an atmosphere unencumbered by adults the things they have learned or have imagined about social relationships."

Important as the adolescent peer group is, not all of the professional adolescent watchers agree that it's all-powerful. Good news for mothers and fathers: Some of the newer studies of "normal" adolescents, such as those conducted by Daniel and Judith B. Offer of the University of Chicago, show that you're important, too. In fact, such studies reveal that you have far more influence on your children in comparison to their adolescent peer groups than you give yourself credit for.

The Offers cite as proof not only their own careful look at adolescent development but also other, similar studies. Then how did the myth of the peer group as so mighty a force come about? In their book *From Teenage to Young Manhood* the Offers give this reasonable explanation: When children become adolescents, the power their parents have over them is considerably reduced. Parents sense this, realize their children are separating from them, and see (maybe for the first time) that these offspring of theirs are capable of taking care of themselves. So they suddenly take note of their children's peer group, "an influence that the parents had no real need to recognize in the past." And what happens then? The adolescent peer group becomes "a reference group for expressions of dissatisfaction or satisfaction with their offspring."

In other words, from then on they invest the peer group with more power than it may really have, and also use it as a focus for blame whenever their teenage children do anything troubling.

Adolescents vary in the way they need and use their peers —their friends. Some are much more intense about it than others are, and for a longer period. In general, these are the more insecure children, and the ones who don't have a good relationship with their parents. It's also an inescapable fact that when children form close friendships with boys or girls their parents deem "poor influences," they *choose* to do so. In all honesty, then, the key question becomes not "Why is that other child corrupting my own?" but "Why is my child drawn to the corrupter?"

Typically, the more rebellious young people are, the more likely they are to drop all their old friends—their "straight" friends—and spend increasing amounts of time with the others. The reasons are fairly obvious. Not feeling straight any more, they feel out of place with the old crew; they don't have much in common any more, they don't have that much to talk about. Also, while they tend to profess contempt for their former friends who know nothing about the "real" world, this is defensive in part—they sense or realize that these friends who aren't into drugs or cutting or splitting from home are looking at *them* a little strangely now.

Who's Responsible Now?

Some rebellious adolescents with troublesome consciences take the clear-cut role of *followers* as they perform destructive or self-destructive acts. That is, their consciences won't permit them to initiate such acts, but by some perverse and peculiar logic they feel absolved of guilt, as it were, if they merely go along with somebody else who has done the initiating and planning.

Joanna is like that. This fifteen-year-old and her friends used her house as a regular meeting place after school, while both her parents were working. They played the stereo at full blast and smoked joints in the back yard. The neighbors were dismayed; one of them finally talked to Joanna's parents.

There was a confrontation between Joanna and her parents; she denied everything but then agreed to tone things down. In reality, though, the resulting quiet merely camouflaged the teenagers' mounting outrage at the tattletale neighbor, and Joanna and her pals plotted revenge. Finally, they tore up a patch of grass in his back yard and put dog feces in his mailbox.

The furious neighbor again contacted Joanna's mother and father, who naturally accused her and her friends of the vandalism. At first Joanna flatly denied having had anything to do with it and acted offended that her mother and father could even think such a thing. After much more talk she broke down and admitted having taken part—and said in genuinely self-righteous tones, as though to rid herself of all responsibility, "But I wasn't the one who thought it up. It was Regina. She worked the whole thing out, and I guess the rest of us got caught up in it."

"But why *did* you get involved?" Joanna's mother persisted.

"Oh, that Regina—she sometimes gets crazy ideas and it's hard to say no," was Joanna's quick reply.

To which her mother weakly said, "I wish you wouldn't be friends with her."

Not being directly held responsible for her own actions, Joanna keeps using her friends as an excuse. In actuality, of course, whether Joanna herself initiated the vandalism or merely went along, the responsibility for her participation was not Regina's, but her own.

What the "Undesirables" Offer

Friends considered poor influences offer excitement—a lightning rod for the electric crackle of anger the rebellious child so strongly feels inside himself. More than that, they offer *acceptance* and *intimacy*.

Not long ago a couple of Texas researchers, Spyros Catechis and Joe Carbonari, took a look at fifty families with children ranging from sixteen to eighteen. As they reported in a paper delivered at a meeting sponsored by the American Association of Psychiatric Services for Children, Inc., half of the total group of children had already been labeled "delinquent" because of behavior that landed them in a court-appointed treatment setting. The other half, far from being officially delinquent, were selected as living reasonably tranquil lives in suburban Houston. Catechis and Carbonari uncovered some crucial differences in the way the two kinds of families functioned:

•The delinquent youngsters—unlike the nondelinquent ones—saw a good deal of inconsistency in the way their parents communicated with them.

•The delinquent ones—unlike the others—saw the same kind of inconsistency in the way their mothers and fathers related to each other.

•In healthy families, "the father may depend on the mother for certain things, the mother may depend on the father, and both of them may depend on the children for some things," whereas this kind of functioning—this "collaborative, cooperative effort"—seemed to be missing in the families with delinquent youngsters.

•In the families with delinquent children, the parents

seemed to have a lot of trouble expressing feelings—feelings of being weak or scared sometimes, but positive feelings, too. A sense of closeness was missing. And the delinquent youngsters said they felt this lack.

When young people who consistently commit troubling acts are asked what they get from those friends to whom their parents object so much, a common answer is: "They accept me and they love me." It's not a flip answer; it happens to be the truth as they feel it. Experiencing themselves as different from the inhabitants of the straight world—not only in their actions but in their thoughts and feelings as well—they're most comfortable with others more or less like them. At home, in school, and among their straight neighbors, they feel disliked, unloved, criticized, undesirable. Collectively, in their little clique, these young outcasts from mainstream society do welcome, support, and love each other. That's all genuine. On the other hand, given their overall instability and impulsiveness, they're not consistent in their mutual support systems. So in time events occur to make them feel individually betrayed, to make them choose sides, and to make them give vent to angry passions. For instance, a girl will suddenly seduce her best friend's boyfriend and sleep with him. Such events create vicious rents in their little social systems.

PARENTAL INTERFERENCE

All adolescents, whether or not they're highly rebellious, hate to have their parents meddle in their friendships. That's sacred territory, as far as they're concerned; Hands Off! *They* chose those friends, and they have a strong sense of identification with them. They don't want their parents to limit their friendships in any way. Above all, they don't want their mothers and fathers telling them which friends are okay and which ones are undesirable and should be dropped. To this critical advice, most teenagers react with outrage.

In the case of highly rebellious young persons, such feelings are intensified precisely because it's in their cliques that they get the kind of affirmation and support they feel they're not getting at home. Very bitter arguments can be precipitated when rebels' parents tell them to drop certain friends. They insist that those friends are *not* undesirable, that parental prejudice is at work, stemming from the parents' own particular view of things.

In fact, family service workers say, sometimes there is considerable truth to these assertions. Mothers and fathers are not always free of bias when passing judgment on their children's friends. Without necessarily being in the least aware of it, they may resent the fact that their children are separating from them, may look for scapegoats, and may find them in those friends of their children's. If there are some young people around your son or daughter whom you thoroughly dislike and distrust—who, you're convinced, are bad news for your own children, think about it as carefully and honestly as you can. Do you resent at least a little the fact that, more and more, your adolescent children are leading lives independent of you? Are you being as fair and objective as you can be? If, after some searching self-examination the answer is still a resounding *yes,* bear certain realities in mind:

• The moment you openly declare your dislike or distrust for a certain child, your own offspring will likely declare undying loyalty to that very child.

• The moment you order your child to stop seeing a particular friend you're apt to get a flat, angry refusal or, worse, a sullen "Okay," which is a promise your child has no intention of keeping. Children do see forbidden friends on the sly. It happens all the time.

Fact: In general, children are much more apt to drop undesirable friends on their own sooner or later, when they make their own discovery of that undesirability, than when parents try to push them into it. The less you interfere the better the chance that the friendship will run its course. But if you feel so strongly about the destructiveness of a particular friendship that you *must* protest, a simple, quiet declaration will suffice to let your child know how you feel. And will affirm that you're deeply concerned about his or her welfare. If, despite the risk of prolonging rather than shortening the friendship, you're intent on making such a declaration, counselors suggest you keep the following in mind:

• Be as straightforward and detailed in your objections as you possibly can be.

• Avoid "badmouthing"—saying things like, "That's a rotten kid," or, "I knew when I first laid eyes on her that she wasn't any good."

• Don't badger your child to end the friendship.

• Make it clear that you realize the ultimate decision about the friendship rests with your child.

How to Say No to Your Children's Friends

Some mothers and fathers go to extremes—if they're not being inflexible with regard to their children's friends, they let them get away with far too much. Both extremes stem from the same source, and you can guess what it is—parental insecurity. In other words, mothers and fathers who deep down feel they lack "authority" as parents tend to be super-rigid or super-permissive not only with their children but with their children's friends as well. They go the one way in the hope of achieving control, the other way because they don't really think they can effect any control at all. Too, some parents aren't sure how much authority they have a right to assert over the conduct of their children's friends, even in their own homes.

Family counselors are unequivocal in stating that you have

every right to expect your children's friends to behave acceptably whether they're in your home or on an outing with you, to obey rules even as you expect your own children to obey them. To do otherwise is to condone and encourage further misbehavior; kids do, after all, egg each other on.

But how do you get through to your children's friends if they won't listen? And if your own child won't listen, either? This is the predicament Christina, a single parent, was in. She had a rule about marijuana, the usual one that parents try to impose—no pot smoking at home. Yet her daughter Cassie and Cassie's friends were obviously smoking from time to time. When she asked them to stop they always said, "Sure," then blatantly disregarded her. Christina felt helpless; she didn't know what to do. She kept getting angry with Cassie and Cassie's crowd—but then, her anger spent, she walked away from the situation. One day she stumbled on one of Cassie's friends cleaning some marijuana. She said, "My God, what are you doing?" and then, without waiting for an answer, quickly left the room.

Christina was obviously not dealing constructively with the troublesome situation. This often happens when parents have problems with their children's friends. If you find echoes of Christina's predicament in your own home, consider the following:

· Maybe you're not being clear in what you expect from your children's friends; try to make your points as precisely as possible.

· Maybe you're not being as firm as you might be; be as coolly and pleasantly determined as you possibly can. Don't leave room for doubt or give the impression that the children have options available to them when in fact you definitely want them to do, or not do, something. For instance, if you want them to clean up after cooking in your kitchen, don't say, "I hope you'll clean everything up after you're through cooking and eating," because that tends to convey that they have a choice. Instead, say, "Please clean up everything in the kitchen before you leave." Clear, direct, no ambiguity.

• Maybe you're not being consistent. If, for instance, you strenuously object to the stereo being turned on full blast one day, don't simply shrug it off the next. Inconsistency confuses the young people, understandably enough, and lessens their willingness to take you seriously.

But what if you are clear and firm and consistent, yet your children's friends still refuse to take you seriously and continue to cause problems and discomfort in your home—what then? Then, though you can't force a friendship to end, you may have no choice but to forbid a particular friend of your child's, the one whose behavior is too often disruptive, to come to your house. Counselors suggest that these circumstances justify such a prohibition:

• The friend deliberately breaks things.

• The friend steals things from your home.

• Your home is being used as a cache for objects stolen elsewhere.

• The friend consistently violates house rules.

• The friend is verbally abusive to you or any other member of your family.

• The friend is physically abusive to you or anyone else in your family.

The distinction between trying to force a friendship's end and barring a particular youth from your home is, or should be, clear. It's your home as well as your child's. You have a right to some tranquillity, to keep your property intact, and to be treated respectfully.

This is what Christina eventually discovered. Now she says, "They didn't listen about the pot smoking, there were things missing, I had to put special locks on closets—I finally learned I couldn't dodge issues, they'd just get messier. Today if I caught a chum of my daughter's cleaning marijuana in my house I'd take it and destroy it. Today I know that accepting *all* my daughter's friends, regardless of who they are and what they're up to, isn't a loving thing to do, either on her behalf or mine. To pretend not to know what's going on is, I now know, avoiding reality. If they're smoking in my house and I turn my head away, they have only two choices—to think I'm stupid or to have no respect for me. That's bad—for them, for Cassie, and for me. Now I tell them what's permitted and what isn't, and I mean it, and they have a lot more respect for me. I have a lot more respect for myself."

14. When the Marriage Is Affected

Sol and Jan were an especially close couple. Even after eighteen years of marriage they were still devoted to each other, still felt romantic about each other, and still preferred spending as much time as they could alone together to doing things with other people. They also thought they had a rich family life; they deeply loved their only child, Vera, and she never gave them cause for concern. Never, that is, until she turned sixteen and became both sexually and emotionally involved with a young man a few years older than she, a black musician.

Neither Sol nor Jan could stand Vera's boyfriend, which precipitated a number of increasingly stormy scenes. She accused them of being racist; they insisted their dislike stemmed from his manners—rude; from his values—he was a high-school dropout and proud of it; and from the way he supported himself—they were pretty sure he was dealing in drugs. At any rate, when her parents refused to allow the young man to sleep over, Vera proceeded to run away from home. As if Sol and Jan were not shocked and incredulous enough at that, she stayed away, dropping out of school herself and establishing

147

housekeeping with her boyfriend, which shocked and pained
them even more.

In the days, weeks, and finally months that followed
Vera's departure, Sol and Jan became increasingly tortured.
Over and over they discussed with each other—and, to a lesser
extent, with a few trusted friends—the reasons why she ran.
Was it solely because of her passion for this boy they loathed?
Did their loathing become the trigger for this sudden, angry
rebelliousness? Or had she stored up grievances over the years
until, sparked by the boyfriend issue, they sprang to ugly life?
Was it maybe Sol and Jan's specially close union that was the
real cause of her upset—despite the love they thought they'd
given her? Did she feel like an outsider with them?

Possibilities considered, possibilities discarded (how *could*
she have felt like an outsider? It couldn't be that). The point
is that throughout the ordeal Sol and Jan were there for each
other. Each felt equally the anguish and the bitterness—but
really never once, in all that terrible time, did they lash out at
each other. When one was blue, the other was there to say
some cheering words. When one raged with the unfairness of
it all, the other was there to soothe. They were each other's
unwavering support.

These two marital partners are quite real—but also quite
unusual. Their marriage remained as strong and sound as ever
while they were trying to adjust to, and make sense of, their
daughter's abandonment of them. And it does happen in other
cases, in marriages hardly marked by such unwavering ardor,
that the sorrow produced by a child's intense rebelliousness
brings the two spouses closer together. But that, too, is far from
the common situation. More commonly the marital partners
have been in conflict with each other prior to the outbreak of
adolescent rebellion; if they haven't been openly fighting, they
have been acting out their resentments toward each other in
a covert way. When the turmoil begins, and continues, their
hostilities surface. And even when a history of conflict hasn't

shadowed the marriage, it's much more to be expected that the parents of a hostile, rebellious child will attack rather than support each other.

This is very evident as one observes couples attending their first FA meeting. Often the two parents arrive looking stiff and angry. They may refrain from looking at each other or sit apart. They may try to attack each other. They admit their marriage has been deeply affected by the chaotic situation they're in. When a child's rebellion brings prolonged turmoil to a family, talk of marital separation becomes more common, and some couples actually do separate and divorce.

This escalation of marital tension is not surprising in view of the stressful things that are occurring. Both partners have become so worried, so tense, so upset. They're angry about what's happening and rail against the fates that have made it happen to *them*. Their limits of tolerance shorten drastically. They become snappish with each other. They blame themselves for the sad and sorry happenings, but they don't stop there. Sooner or later they look around for somebody else to share the blame—and blame each other.

"When children manifest serious behavior problems, some blaming—one parent blaming the other for what's going on—is inevitable," according to psychotherapist Jan Robinson. "You might almost say it's normal. It's 'abnormal,' so to say, when it's a rigid kind of blaming—when you say it's all your spouse's fault and don't look at yourself or take other factors into consideration."

So it is that a mother lashes out at her husband, the rebellious girl's father, with a very familiar complaint: "If you'd only been home more, instead of always off on your business trips, leaving all the child-rearing responsibility to me!" So it is that this father lashes right back: "If you'd only been stricter with her, none of this would have happened!"

So it is that another mother snaps accusingly at her husband, the troubled son's father: "You should have let him know who's boss. But he was the apple of your eye. When he was a basketball star it was *your* star that was shining—you were so proud!—and you didn't dare speak up for fear of alienating him." And the father hurls back his own little tidbit: "You were right in there all the time, trying to tell me what to say, sitting up on Mount Olympus watching the show, trying to manage the puppets, but never really getting involved yourself!"

Later on, a lot wiser, their marriages on a better footing, some parents realize the folly of playing the game of accuse and counteraccuse. This comes now from Sheila, the mother whose son, Roger, had gone AWOL from the Navy: "I think this is the way we were taught—'Who spilled the milk?'—rather than 'Who's going to clean it up?' We have to cast blame. It was so difficult for so long to blame my poor son, because he was so sick and miserable. So it must be Pete's—my husband's—fault. I'd dream up anything. I'd blame him for not doing anything, for not realizing what was going on, for not understanding. For not being loving enough." And Pete now says, "I didn't go to Families Anonymous meetings because *I* had a problem, I drove her down because *she* had a problem. She —I then thought—was making too much of the situation our son was in. So I was perfectly willing to go to FA meetings— to straighten *her* out!"

Steve and Beth, who were perfectly willing to let Ron, their younger son, spend a little time in juvenile hall when he was caught shoplifting, are another example. Remembering the awful times when she and Steve were constantly bellowing at each other and on the verge of splitting, Beth could later say, "I always saw my husband as the strong one, as the head of the family. Whenever there's been a problem, all I had to do was turn to him and he could handle it. But when this thing came up with the older boy, and then the younger one started acting up, too, he had no more control over things than I did. That angered me. Why couldn't he do something about this? One night I was outside the house, peering into the older boy's bedroom through the sheer curtains, and I could see him and his friends. My boy had a syringe in his hand and it looked like he was giving somebody an injection. So I came back into the house and I was really frightened. I said, 'Do something, do something, he's in there giving somebody a shot—do something.' And my husband sat there with the newspaper in his hand, petrified. And I thought, 'My God, he was an intelligent man when I married him; what's happened? He just doesn't seem to be able to do anything.' Well, that was so unfair, we were both in the same boat, not knowing what to do to save the situation. I didn't have any right to expect more of him than I had of myself. Finally, after a lot of struggles, we've reached an accommodation: I no longer expect anything of him, he no longer expects anything of me. I do what I have to do, he does what he has to do."

Casting blame is always a most unhelpful if not destructive approach to problem solving. There are other things wrong with it. To cast blame is to say, "It's all your fault," which is invariably a simplistic and fallacious view of a situation. And, in the context of two parents and a troubled and troubling child, everybody involved shares in the responsibility.

The point has been made before, but it's worth repeating here: Everybody is one hundred percent involved, even when it doesn't seem so on the surface. Example: A somewhat harsh, punitive father causes his child a considerable amount of grief. How's the boy's gentle, quiet mother in any way responsible? As Jan Robinson points out, "She can't or won't give the child appropriate discipline on her own, leaving that aspect of parenting entirely to her husband. Also, she can't or won't stand up to him when he's being too harsh."

Another example: A possessive, overprotective mother offers a smothering kind of love to her child. Ms. Robinson says, "When you look at such a situation initially, the father comes out smelling like a rose, but in fact he has allowed it to go on and on." He can't or won't protect his child from his wife's possessive love.

Counselors suggest: If casting blame is to some extent inevitable, that doesn't mean it inevitably has to have a corrosive effect. You *can* keep it in check.

If accusations are being hurled in your family, try to understand where they're coming from. Both you *and* your spouse are tired, frustrated, angry, and unhappy—to say the least. Both of you wish desperately that things would be otherwise. Blaming is a way of giving vent to all those feelings, of releasing some of the inner tension—of reducing self-blame. Keep reminding yourself that all the storms raging within you also rage with equal force in your partner. If you find yourself starting to accuse, try very hard—consciously—to hold yourself in check. If you're the target for blame, try very hard—consciously—to understand where the accusations are coming from, and not counterattack. Counterattacking will just increase the levels of hostility and tension, whereas calmly and firmly asking your partner to stop is much more apt to produce at least an armistice.

Some veterans of those I-blame-you, you-blame-me fights say they became much less accusatory when they deliberately stopped accusing and looked at their own actions once more. One such mother recalls, "There's nothing like taking your own inventory again, looking at your own behavior honestly and clearly, to give you a little humility. And there's nothing like a little humility to put a damper on your urge to blame somebody else."

Clearly, such advice is easier to give than to carry out in times of great stress. Nevertheless, those mothers and fathers who do try it say it works; it helps them to act more and more as a parental unit, which in turn helps them to achieve their avowed goal of making life more peaceable.

OTHER TRAPS TO WATCH FOR

Parents who have been through it all point to three other mother-father patterns of interaction that keep them from acting together, as a unit:

Two against one. Feeling powerless but needing power, highly rebellious boys and girls often try to conquer and divide —to get one parent to side with them against the other. One common trick is to get one parent to agree to keep a secret from the other. Stan tells his mother, "Listen, I got into trouble in school today, and I want to tell you about it, but you've got to promise not to tell Dad; you know how he flies off the handle whenever anything happens." His mother replies, "All right, dear, I promise." Instantly, she has become Stan's ally against his father, which means the two parents can't act in concert in dealing with the situation, which means it can't be dealt with effectively. She never intended to be in collusion with Stan against his father, but that's the way it works out.

Your judgment doesn't count. There's a different way in which a child and one parent become allies against the other parent. This is how it works: One parent makes a decision the child doesn't like, the child goes to the other parent for the desired decision, and the other parent obliges, going counter to the first one's decision. Example: Patricia wants to borrow the family car. Because she cut classes for the third time in a week and then swore at her mother when they had a row about it, her mother says no. Patricia appeals to her father, he succumbs, and it's yes, she can use the car. He may know that his wife said no but feel that it was unfair, or he may not even have bothered to check with her. Such maneuvers evoke a great deal of anger in the spouses whose decisions have been countermanded. They complain, with justice, of being constantly undermined by their mates.

I'll be the referee. This is otherwise known as "getting in the middle." A father who finally learned to remove himself from the arena describes it beautifully: "Whenever my wife and daughter fought—which was a lot of the time—I'd try to smooth things over. I'd jump right in there, the professional arbitrator who wanted to make nicey-nicey with everyone. Sometimes my wife asked me to step in, sometimes my daughter—and sometimes, if I wasn't asked, I'd do it on my own. So I'd calm them down, but by that time I was upset and exhausted—and sore at them both. 'Why don't you handle your own battles?' I'd tell my wife illogically, but there I'd be, plunging right in. Well, it took me a long time to learn that the more I stepped in, the more I was helping them to keep on with those fierce confrontations. What finally helped me stop playing the mediator was the reports I kept getting from all the people in my family—that when I wasn't around, my wife and daughter didn't fight like that."

How to Work Together

These examples come from parents whose discord began or was aggravated during very disturbing and stressful times involving a troubled child and who flirted with the idea of splitting, but, after a lot of hard work, at last learned to work together, appreciate each other, and give each other much-needed support. The examples may not necessarily fit your situation—and you may not agree with the solutions worked out here—but they do suggest some alternatives for parents who haven't been acting as a unit.

•A mother who took upon herself most or all of the responsibility in dealing with her drug-addicted son—"My husband always said he was too busy with work or insisted I did a much better job of handling things"—now isn't so quick to step in. "I've learned to let go. I *do* do a much better job of it sometimes, but then I resent my husband for dumping it all on me. Now, much of the time, if Kevin calls with a problem,

I'll say, 'Talk to your father.' Sometimes he doesn't even discuss it with me any more, just says, 'Hi, Mom,' and asks for his dad. At first my husband was reluctant to assume this responsibility, but when I said I wasn't going to do it any more he said okay. And now things are much better between us."

•The father of a chronic runaway daughter says he used to act too quickly where she was concerned, making decisions in her favor thoughtlessly, simply because she asked him to, without consulting his wife. "For instance, my daughter would ask for an extra night out, I'd say yes, and later discover that my wife had already turned her down, or would have turned her down had she been asked, because the girl had been acting so obnoxiously. So then my daughter would be out that extra night, she got what she wanted, but my wife and I would have hard feelings about it. Now I've learned that I don't have to decide things right then—I can take ten. Now I touch base with my wife and we don't let our daughter manipulate us. The other day she called me at the office, wanting something, and I said, 'I'll have to talk it over with your mother first.' She said, a bit angrily, 'The two of you can't decide anything any more without the other.' And I said, 'That's right. For the first time in our lives we're deciding together—so we can't blame each other.'"

•Another man said he and his wife acted too quickly in a different way. They made crisis decisions involving their son together, but on the spur of the moment, in the midst of the excitement, and in front of the rebellious child, who was right there urging them to decide. "Often, feeling pushed like that, we'd do the wrong thing. Then we'd be angry and blame each other," the father explained. "Now we don't let ourselves be pushed. We talk things over when things are calmer and we're by ourselves. What comes out of it is much more constructive, and we're working together, really trying to dope things out."

•Yet a different couple talked about their crisis times, when they were so immersed in problems they forgot their roles as husband and wife. Only when they were on the verge of separating did they get in touch with their loving feelings toward each other again, pull back, and say, "Hey, what's going on here?" Now they remember to work at their marriage, too —to be as open and honest and caring with each other as they can be. Now the wife says, "I can remember both of us being awake in the middle of the night, walking the floor, talking about divorce. Today we're able to face any and every problem that comes up." Her husband adds, "All we have to do is start with the premise that we love each other, realizing how important that is. And putting away little hurts, little grudges—those grudges we'd hold on to. If something bothers us now, we can talk about it and get it out of the way in a minute or two. It's taking a lot of effort, but we have a much better life together now—despite our son's poor circumstances—than we ever had before."

15. Special Problems: Drugs, Sex, Running Away, Violence

Drug Abuse—Telltale Signs

Jeannette, her mother says, went from marijuana to uppers and downers, from pills to LSD, finally culminating her drug experiences with one wild, scary encounter with "angel dust." That one made her suicidal and she very nearly succeeded in doing away with herself; in fact, she had to be hospitalized for a brief period. Recollecting the events, Jeannette's mother says, "For a long time I thought I had something to do with Jeannette's erratic behavior, that somehow I was causing it. I just didn't think of drugs at all. It hasn't been part of our culture. How are we, how are parents, to know?"

Good question. Parents have not been educated to recognize the signs of drug abuse or drug addiction in their children. But giveaway signs are there if one knows how to look for them. Mothers and fathers who have been through the drug abuse mill with their children say that the following signs are pretty good indicators of drug abuse or addiction:

• Parents' prescription medicines—especially tranquilizers and sleeping pills—mysteriously disappear.

• The adolescent starts a new habit—burning incense in her or his room. Maybe the child is meditating or just loves the smell of incense. Often, though, burning incense is used to cover up the distinctive aroma of marijuana.

•Another one or two new habits may appear: wearing sunglasses (to hide dilated pupils) and/or wearing long sleeves all the time, even on the hottest days (to hide needle marks on arms).

•There's a sharp change in friendships; old friends, straight friends, are dropped in favor of young people who are on drugs, just hang around, have no discernible goals, and sneer at authority.

•There's a sharp change in clothes—from neat to sloppy.

•The child's speech becomes slurred.

•Sleeping and energy patterns change—the child becomes listless or sleeps a lot during the day, but is quite restless at night.

•Sudden mood shifts—from normal to angry or highly provocative—are sometimes triggered by marijuana and other drugs.

•There are repeated attempts to borrow money (to be used in buying drugs).

•Salable objects mysteriously disappear from the home (sold to get money for drugs).

DRUG ABUSE—HOW TO HELP THE YOUNG ADDICT

Some parents are so uptight about the use of drugs they confuse use with abuse. Emotionally healthy adolescents may use drugs—principally pot and alcohol—the way adults do; that is, casually, intermittently. These healthy young people want to grow, develop, master the tasks, and gain the skills peculiar to adolescence; they don't want to be zonked out of their minds, slaves to a mood-altering substance. Even if they do go through a brief period of more intense use, they soon reject it. However, there is a hazard even for the better-balanced youths: some, not really wanting to do more than experiment, nevertheless take more and more of such substances and become hooked without realizing that's what's happening to them.

Emotionally troubled adolescents go at drugs in a different way. They may claim they use drugs only for kicks. In reality, because they don't feel adequate to meet stress head on, to work out clear-headed solutions for themselves (or to accept things as they are), they grab at anything that offers them an escape from their problems. It becomes a relief from the pain and tension they're experiencing.

The best solution for parents of young drug addicts is to search out effective drug rehabilitation programs—either day programs or residential ones, depending on the situation—and get their children into such programs. But most of the time this approach works out well only if the young person is motivated to go. Some youths are; many are not. Like alcoholics of any age, many deny they have a problem at all, and it is quite difficult to engage them. Either they run away or they stick it out for the duration but don't really stop using drugs (if it's a day program) or return to drug use soon after being released (if it's a residential program). At least it may be helpful to parents to find out what they can—to consult with an expert in drug rehabilitation, either in private practice or in a drug rehab program. (See the following chapter for a fuller discussion of this topic). Some drug programs also run parent groups, so as to give mothers and fathers a chance to vent their feelings about their addicted children and also to work on ways of relating more effectively to those children. The principle of "changing yourself" is ever important.

What if you try and try to change, yet your son Jake (say) continues to choose to use drugs, chooses not to work on the problem or even see it as a problem, and chooses to insist that he has a right to live his life as he pleases? At a Families Anonymous meeting in Los Angeles not long ago, a guest speaker addressed himself to that problem. He was twenty-three years old and had been a heroin addict from shortly after his sixteenth birthday until he was well past twenty. He told the assembled parents how and why he got on the habit, described in unsparing detail how he stole and passed bad checks to support the habit, and how he lived, on and off, the raw, degrading, youth-sapping street life. Suddenly he pointed to his own mother and father, a well-groomed middle-aged couple who had been listening intently. "I didn't recover," he stated with intense earnestness, "until you two got off my back!"

Many parents of recovered addict sons and daughters would emphatically agree with that young man's remarks. They recall being on their children's backs all the time, wanting them to get off drugs, wanting them to head for college or make the grades or be popular or get jobs. As one such mother puts it, "We got caught in the when-are-you-ing trap—'When are you going to do this, When are you going to do that?'" All of it to no avail. They remember how, for such a long time, they couldn't let go, couldn't stop lecturing, pleading, cajoling, crying, or bribing—and how they got nothing for their sincere, desperate, compulsive efforts except hostile comebacks and broken promises. They recall doing what they thought was the right parental thing to do in the face of their addicted children's desperate needs: feeding them, sheltering them, bailing them out of jail, making good on their bounced checks. Sometimes they used a kind of benign blackmail—"We'll help you out of this trouble if you agree to get into a drug rehabilitation program"—only to have them drop out of these programs or run away from them. And keep on, keep on, keep on using drugs.

Finally, they recall how they at last came to believe the catchy saying that's popular among some families whose children have gone through heavy, horrendous drug experiences: "They only get better when they run out of people, places, and things." Meaning: It's only when the drug addict can no longer find anyone—including his parents—to help him in any way, when he's completely out of resources, that he may first decide to confront himself and his situation realistically. It's only then that he may decide to help himself out of that situation. It's only then that he's motivated to get better. It's only then that drug rehabilitation centers, therapy, or any other program of assistance really works.

This, at any rate, has been the experience of most of these parents. Obviously, there are exceptions. There are young addicts who do allow themselves to be helped by their parents. Some others refuse to get help on their own even when there no longer is anyone around whom they can tap for a loan, a meal, or a bed. They're lost, lost souls; lost, perhaps, forever. But enough addicted children do respond once they're no longer rescued to give validity to that catchy, seemingly harsh slogan about running out of people, places, and things.

A father in Minneapolis, who insists that that's how it happened with his son, remarks, "As long as their parents are there, they can't get well. They go through all their friends and know their parents are the last ones—but when their parents say no, when they can no longer con their parents, the last ones on their list, they have to face facts. Oh, how they do try to con. They'll be angry, they'll play on our guilt and our sympathy, and when they've lost that sympathy, there's no other way to go. It happened with my boy and with the kids of some other parents I know. My boy—here was a kid who'd conned everybody—his friends, grandparents, uncle . . . finally only his mother and I were left. And then even his mother had had enough of him; only his father was left. And at last his father collected his belongings in a couple of paper bags and put them outside the door. He was seventeen. Now that kid of mine is a counselor in a drug program."

SEXUAL PROMISCUITY—WHAT IT IS AND ISN'T

How mothers and fathers react to their children's burgeoning sexuality depends on their own attitudes towards sex —how comfortable they are with it, how much they enjoy their own sex lives, and how free they've been in passing along accurate sex information to their children. There are parents who are accepting—even delighted—when their children reach sexual maturity; in a sense they see sex as being "handed" from generation to generation. There are parents who, having led unsatisfying sex lives of their own, either make fun of or derive vicarious pleasure from their adolescent children's sexual play. There are parents who are so uncomfortable with (or fearful of) sex that they react grimly to any sign of erotic feeling on their children's part. There are parents who think all adolescents run sexually wild if a tight lid isn't kept on their erotic impulses—that a French kiss is already halfway down the road to sexual promiscuity. (They're like those other nervous parents who so readily equate the occasional use of pot with real drug addiction.)

In essence, what may seem like sexual promiscuity in a child may not necessarily be so. Sex play per se, even sexual intercourse per se, on the part of a teenager doesn't realistically constitute promiscuity. What does? Sandy Kagan, of the American Institute of Family Relations, offers the following criteria:

•Sexually promiscuous teenagers are compulsive about sex; it's always uppermost in their thoughts.

•Whenever possible they try to translate thought into action; they're constantly involved in sexual activity.

•Sex is the only way they can relate to members of the opposite sex.

•Peer pressure is an important factor in determining how soon an adolescent has sex. If the crowd is having sex, many young people feel they too have to have it, whereas if they're in a crowd that doesn't have a strong focus on sex it becomes easier to hold off. But the motivating factor in sexual promiscuity goes much deeper than peer pressure. The sexually promiscuous girl, for instance, may unconsciously think, "I'm nothing, I'm no one, and this is the only way I can keep a boy." A sexually promiscuous boy may say to himself, "If I don't screw around like the other guys they'll think I'm scared or a fag."

• Physical development is a factor. Some children develop more rapidly than others. If physical urgency for sex is present, rebellious children might be more inclined to use their bodies in rebelling.

• When there's a sexually repressive atmosphere at home, some adolescents with a need to rebel have a ready-made weapon with which to beat their parents. As Ms. Kagan says, "Children seem to have an innate ability to zoom in on what will drive Mommy and Daddy bananas. It's an unconscious thing, or they learn it when they're so young they're not even aware of it."

This might be especially true for girls, though both girls and boys can be sexually promiscuous. The sexual double standard is such that most parents (except highly religious ones) are really far more concerned about their daughters' sexual activity than about their sons', which is why the examples chosen here largely pertain to girls.

• The father's attitude toward women can also be an important factor prompting a girl to become sexually promiscuous. If the father sees women as sexual objects—if basically he only relates to them sexually rather than as persons—the daughter learns she has to come on in a strong sexual way with boys in order to be noticed.

Many sexually promiscuous teenagers confuse sex with emotional intimacy. They wind up in bed with most or all of their dates, have brief and unsatisfying affairs with them, and are left feeling empty. It's as though they're saying, "I have problems getting close to the opposite sex. Maybe if we have sex together we'll be close." Many girls have troubled relationships with their fathers and go from boy to boy, using sex as a way of getting the protection and understanding they don't feel they're getting at home.

Sexual Promiscuity—What to Avoid, How to Help

Sexual experimentation (not necessarily intercourse) is a well-nigh inevitable facet of adolescence. Experimentation means exploring the social as well as physical facets of a relationship. It means going steady, perhaps, feeling the pangs of "undying love," building new relationships on the ashes of the last "undying" one, observing oneself (learning about oneself) sexually and emotionally. It's a milestone on the road to mature love. As a parent you can encourage or hinder a healthy psychosexual development in your child. If you unwittingly hinder it, you may help to bring on the very promiscuity you don't want to see happen. Here's what to avoid:

•Showing feelings of jealousy or possessiveness when your child begins to date.

•Being competitive with your children's dates (for instance, the father who downgrades his daughter's boyfriends, and the mother who downgrades her son's girl friends, are showing competitiveness).

•Being in collusion with your child around the issue of sex. To give an example relating to girls: Fathers, Ms. Kagan observes, seem to have a harder time of it than mothers accepting the fact that their daughters are having sexual intercourse. It's not uncommon for a mother, therefore, to hide from her husband the fact that their daughter is sleeping with a boy. But if this becomes the family pattern, the mother is taking on a tremendous load. "She's assuming complete responsibility for what's happening with the daughter," Ms. Kagan says, "and has no one to share it with." In time the father is bound to discover what his "little girl" is doing anyway, and then be doubly angry—because she's having sex and because she and his wife conspired to keep this information from him, making him feel like an outsider.

•Giving a flat no to sex, something on the order of, "If you have sex we'll make life rough for you around here." Many adolescents tend to become all the more rebellious when they're given an absolute prohibition (all the more so if it's backed by a threat). The ones predisposed to rebel then have a ready-made excuse for going on the warpath. Even if they're outwardly acquiescent, they may have sex furtively, simply out of anger. A girl may even become "accidentally" pregnant in response to her anger at her parents.

•Telling the child, "I trust you to do the right thing," then pumping that child for information when she or he returns from dates. This is a clear double message: "I trust you to do the right thing but on the other hand I'm not so sure I really do trust you."

•Conversely, subtly encouraging the child to have a swinging sex life. Some parents who feel extremely frustrated in terms of sex consciously or unconsciously push their children to have the kinds of sex lives they wish they themselves had had.

•There's a fundamental fact of life that parents have to accept as regards their children's sex life: they have no control over it. You can watch your teenage daughter (or son, in rare cases—as has been mentioned) twenty-four hours a day, and still that child will manage to live her own sex life. This fact makes some parents very nervous; their response is to be all the more restrictive, probing, and suspicious—which, obviously, invites nothing but rebellion.

What, then, is the most helpful position you can assume with respect to your child's sexuality in general? Try to weave an atmosphere around sex that's wholesome and accepting. Try to have frank, open talks with your child about sex—about the joys and hazards of sex, the feeling good, the sharing, the learning about oneself and others, the dangers of pregnancy and venereal disease, the hazard of being sexually exploited or abused, and the sexual values by which you live.

You have no real control over your child's sex life—but you do, it's to be assumed, have some moral authority over your child, and you do have certain sexual standards and values you want your child to share. You can't make your child adopt them, but you can express them in a clear, unambiguous way —and live your life in a way that reflects them. For instance, parents who don't want their children to fool around but are themselves promiscuous or unfaithful have a hard time getting their message across.

Let's say you've expressed your values calmly and clearly, but you're not getting through. Your teenager jeers and tells you how old-fashioned you are, how out of touch with modern thinking. What then? Your child may be trying to draw you into a debate. If you do argue with her, she may see you as pressuring her to believe what you believe and be all the more vehement in defending her own very liberal views, the ones so unnerving to you. You don't have to argue. You've spelled out your own position; that's all you mean to do. Even if your child is apparently shutting you off, she's heard you. On some level, even if she seems to reject it, she has to deal with your viewpoint.

If you have a child who *is* sexually promiscuous, that message about your own values either has never been given or hasn't made an impression. It's not apt to make an impression now. What can you do? Review the list of approaches to avoid as listed on the previous pages, and if one or more strike a responsive chord you can take steps to change things. Too, consider the fact that if your daughter is using sex as a way of rebelling, maybe she's doing so to boost a sagging ego or to get the protection and affection she needs. Be less critical, make more of an effort to praise. If you're her father, try giving her more attention and affection than before. She may not want to spend more time with you (for various reasons she may strongly need *not* to be with you so much now, during her adolescence), but it's important for her to know that you do love her and feel protective toward her. She may be willing to try counseling, now or a bit later. Some sexually promiscuous girls resist any form of therapy at first—but if they're not getting what they want through sex and they keep on getting hurt and feeling empty, in time they agree to try it.

RUNAWAY CHILDREN—WHY THEY RUN

Many parents whose children run away tend to see the running as a purely rebellious act. As one mother, member of a southern California FA group, put it, "I thought she took off just to spite me." And another, "My first impulse when John ran off with his girl friend was—'How could you do this to me?' "

In one sense running away is a rebellious act, of course—the child is taking off without permission, a most blatant way of flouting parental authority. Running away also is an act of anger and revenge—*I'll show 'em!*—on the part of teenagers who, rightly or wrongly, feel themselves unloved, unappreciated, misunderstood, or abused at home. Underneath it all, however, the child who runs away—just like the child who attempts to commit suicide—is sending a poignant message: "Pay attention to me—I hurt!"

That hurt may take any number of shapes and forms. Scott ran because he failed math and nearly failed a science course in his junior year in high school; he was afraid of his parents' reaction. Underneath, he felt that his parents weren't really looking at him as a human being but as an extension of themselves who had to perform at consistently high levels to merit their approval and their love. Candy ran away because she thought she was pregnant and couldn't bring herself to tell her parents; she thought, perhaps rightly as they later admitted, that they'd condemn her bitterly. Nancy ran ostensibly because she and her mother were always quarreling about clothes, cleanliness, the condition of her room, and so on. But a lot more was going on in her family; her mother and father were locked in bitter though muted marital conflict, and she couldn't stand the tension. Because many of their fights were about her, she also felt guilty and thought that if she was out of their sight maybe they'd get along better.

Children run from home because they're physically abused, because they feel scapegoated, or because they feel their parents want them to adopt styles of life that don't fit their personalities. As a young runaway, a fourteen-year-old girl, explained, "They wanted me to be them, not me." Many such runaways have been living two lives—ostensibly the kind their parents want them to live and also a secret life, a life carefully hidden from their mothers and fathers, in which they've done what they wanted. When the pressure fostered by having to juggle those two existences became too great, or they were on the verge of being discovered, they split. Many young runaways were convinced that life had to be better "out there" than it was at home; not infrequently they come to see that this is an illusion and that everywhere, even in runaway shelters, people have rules and expectations.

Studies show that in most instances it's a long, slow accumulation of grievances, resentments, and dissatisfactions on both sides of the parent-child relationship that finally prompts the child to run—though the actual decision to take off may be rather sudden. Paradoxically, sometimes it's guilt that drives young people to run away. Regardless of how hostile and resentful they may seem, most highly rebellious boys and girls do feel guilty on some level for the pain and upset they cause, and when this guilt builds up to unmanageable proportions, off they go. At times, seasoned FA parents say, a runaway episode is triggered when a mother or father does something especially nice for a rebellious child. Phoebe, the divorced mother of a sixteen-year-old girl who finally joined Narcotics Anonymous, a self-help group for potheads and other drug addicts, says her daughter ran away twice. The first time was right after she'd slipped and gotten heavily stoned on pot again. The second time, which occurred during Christmas week, she'd had a terrific row with her mother, cursing her and spitting on her, and then, despite this nasty fight, Phoebe bought the girl an expensive dress that she'd promised her. Only a day later the child ran away again; now Phoebe reckons, "I laid more guilt on her by doing something nice for her at a time when I shouldn't have spent a dime on her."

RUNAWAY CHILDREN—NEEDLESS WORRY

When their boys and girls run away, especially for the first time, many mothers and fathers go into a kind of panic. Having no facts on hand at all, not knowing whether their children are in the neighborhood or heading across the country, they immediately jump to some terrible conclusions. Their children have been mugged, beaten, raped. Their children are sick. Their children are dead.

Such thoughts of gloom and doom are really a form of needless torture. In most instances these days, runaways don't run far; most of them stay with friends and return home in a few days. As for those who do elect to travel a considerable distance from home, a growing number of them stay in legitimate, certified runaway shelters.

There has been a great deal of publicity in recent years about runaway girls and boys who survive by prostituting themselves. But, although it's true that thousands of them do try to survive in this harshest of ways, given the hundreds of thousands of teenage runaways, they are very much in the minority. As a staff member of a runaway house in Washington, D.C., put it, "The daughter will run away and the parents immediately assume she's run to California, is living a promiscuous life, and taking all kinds of drugs—when the kid is actually down the street, scared stiff, lonely, maybe living with a friend."

Parents who have been through their children's runaway episodes suggest: Don't project all kinds of horrible fates befalling your runaway when you don't have a shred of information about the child's whereabouts and activities. You'll feel a lot better.

Runaway Children—Handling the Reunion

Most runaway children return home within a few days, but some return only to run again at a later point. The more often they run, the longer they're apt to stay away each successive time. Also, the longer they're on the road each time, the greater the chance that, eventually, they won't return home at all. The first reunion is a very sensitive time. It can set the stage for a better parent-child relationship, or it can be the springboard for repeat episodes.

When your child runs away, you have to deal with a welter of difficult emotions triggered by the inescapable fact that the child has abandoned you. Besides your natural concern, you're bound to feel very hurt, humiliated, angry. Your runaway feels somewhat kindred emotions (for needing to abandon you). In the first flush of the reunion you may all embrace and cry and assure each other that from now on things will get better. For a bit, while all the characters in this poignant family drama are on their best behavior, things *are* better. But if those other feelings aren't dealt with, if the reason for the runaway episode isn't carefully examined, the old familiar patterns will reassert themselves.

As an example, suppose you are a parent of Mike, a run-away who has returned home. Parents and counselors who have had firsthand experience with runaways suggest your consider-ing the following approaches to Mike:

• Avoid pumping him about where he's been or what he's done while he was away. If he wants to tell you, he will; if he doesn't, you're not apt to get the truth anyway, just resent-ment.

• Avoid accusations. "How could you do this to me?" is hardly germane when, in fact, he did it—and, at the time, may have felt compelled to do it.

• Express all your feelings openly and honestly. You *were* very worried about him, presumably. You *were* deeply hurt. You *were* angry—maybe because of all the pain he caused, maybe because he stole some money from you to pay for his bus ticket. But you *do* love him and you *are* glad to have him back. All those feelings deserve expression.

• Listen to him without getting into a quarrel if he has things he wants to express. Some of what he says may be hurting, some may be unfair to you, but consider them as calmly as you can.

• Above all, don't fall into the common trap of viewing the runaway episode as *the* problem, or even Mike himself as the problem for having run away. It's easy to focus on the running because that's the immediate, visible event. But running away is only a symptom of distress. It may not be the best way of handling a situation, but the fact remains that a runaway epi-sode involves the entire family. The child ran away—but it's the family that's in trouble.

• It's sometimes hard for the parties directly involved to sort out the underlying reasons for the child's need to leave home. Some counselors who work with runaways and their families feel that at least a professional consultation or two can be helpful in warding off repeat episodes.

• Not infrequently a youth who runs away once will

threaten to run away again if he doesn't get his own way in something. That threat is partly manipulative, partly an indication that the tensions precipitating the first runaway episode are still present. Counselors suggest: You don't want your child to run away again, but you can't allow yourself to become a doormat, subject to blackmail, either. Say something on the order of, "We don't want you to run away again, but we can't let you threaten us like this. We can't be afraid to correct you or to say no to you when it's necessary."

VIOLENT CHILDREN—WHY THEY HIT, WHAT TO DO

A fifty-three-year-old father tells his fourteen-year-old son that it's past midnight, he's not to go out any more. They exchange words. The father blocks the front doorway. The son, who towers over his father by more than a foot, throws the older man against a wall and stomps out.

A mother and her daughter, the girl in her mid-teens, have a terrific fight. During the thick of it they shake each other in rage. Then the daughter slaps the mother sharply three times across the mouth.

A boy of seventeen wants the keys to his mother's car. She refuses to give them to him. He makes a dive for his mother's purse to get the keys; she tries to stop him. He slams his fist down hard on one of her fingers and it aches so she thinks it might be broken. (It swells but there's no fracture.) She slaps him and he strikes her, knocking her to the floor. Whimpering, dressed only in a nightgown and slippers, she runs out of the house to a telephone booth on the corner and calls her husband. She waits outside, afraid to return home, until he arrives.

Such painful stories related by FA parents make it clear that physical abuse isn't something only parents perpetrate on children. Sometimes boys and girls in their teenage years inflict it on their mothers or fathers as well.

Aggressive impulses are strong in adolescence. The Offers' studies of "normal" adolescent boys show that many of them had lots of trouble coping with anger and hostility—more so than with their sexual impulses. They did lash out at parents, siblings, girl friends, or teachers, but they held their anger to socially acceptable limits. Mainly they coped with aggression through competitive sports.

When aggression goes beyond acceptable limits—when adolescents hit and punch and kick their parents—then such disputes as whether or not to go out after midnight or whether the child is allowed to use the family car are only surface issues. Underneath, stresses psychotherapist Thomas H. Waner, there are "chronic problems of intimacy" between the abusing child and the victim parent. The child feels unloved. The parent probably feels unloved, too. The child wants to make up for his feelings of deprivation by getting special favors or things. The parent, having had endlessly trying times with this unloving child, tries to hold on to a semblance of adult power by withholding that special favor or thing. The child feels like a pawn—like a victim to the parent's whims. In rage and frustration, he lashes out physically.

While fairly common when a child becomes violent against a parent, this pathetic scenario on the basic issues hardly justifies the child's aggression. Waner and other therapists agree that violence should never be allowed or condoned, whether against a parent or a sibling. They offer the following suggestions and observations:

•Children are much more likely to act out their aggressive feelings violently when they see violence displayed, perhaps between the parents, when siblings are allowed to hit each other, or when there's a good deal of verbal abuse in the home.

•Certain drugs—"angel dust" is a prominent example— can induce violent behavior; specifically, they create highly agitated paranoid states.

•Try not to do anything to provoke violence. In retrospect, some parents realize they helped spark aggression by taunting, prodding, or becoming physical themselves. The mother of that seventeen-year-old who knocked her down when she wouldn't let him use her car now knows she should not have slapped him; it was only when she did so that he became so violent. On a subsequent occasion she and he got into a quarrel in his room. He yelled at her and wouldn't let her leave. Again she was frightened, but this time she knew she must do nothing to provoke real violence. As calmly and quietly as she could, she told him that he was scaring her. Pretty soon he calmed down.

• What if one of your children slaps or punches or shoves you to the ground? The child must understand that you have personal boundaries that are inviolate; that physical assault on your body does violence to those boundaries and is totally unacceptable. And if the violence continues? Then you have several options. You can accept the continuing assaults and live your life being intimidated by your child. You can meet violence with violence—which happens in some families where the parent is evenly matched or bigger than the child; predictably, though, that only brings on escalating episodes of physical abuse. You can warn the child that he or she will no longer be able to live at home if the violence continues—and mean it. You can call the police, especially if the child's aggressive impulses get so out of hand that you feel yourself in danger of being really hurt. This, too, some distraught parents have finally done. Lastly, if the child becomes truly homicidal, hospitalization may be the only answer.

Parents who feel they have no choice but to call the police generally find that the police are reluctant to respond; they say that a case such as this is a "domestic matter." When parents persist and prove willing to press charges for assault and battery, the cops may try to make them feel guilty for doing this to their own children. Then many parents back down. But some FA members have persisted and actually filed charges; it was the only alternative, they say, to being beaten up again by one of their own sons or daughters.

Referring to such parents, Waner comments, "One of the scary things about being a parent is that sometimes you have to stand alone in the world. It takes a lot of courage to be a parent because sometimes you have to say, 'This is what I believe; this is what I have to do as regards my kid even if I'm the only one in the neighborhood who does it.' That's a lonely, scary place to be."

OUTSIDE HELP

16. Considering Outside Help

CANDIDATES FOR PSYCHOTHERAPY

If you've sought—or considered seeking—outside help for a troubled adolescent, you know how difficult it can be to make that decision. It means facing up to the realization that the situation has indeed become unmanageable—or, at least, that you can't manage it. It means the shock of guilt—the rush of jumbled thoughts that turn out to become the simple, shocking (but, of course, erroneous) refrain, "It's all my fault." It means another painfully shocking (but just as unrealistic) thought, "Is my child crazy?" It means all kinds of nameless fears—*How much will it cost? What's going to happen? What will be uncovered?*—that for the moment must remain largely unanswered.

You also hear disturbing stories of children—or parents and children—who were in lengthy and expensive treatment at the end of which the young patients were no better off than before. One FA family, for example, talks bitterly of spending $60,000 in one year on the best psychiatric care they could get for their daughter, only to have her remain as disturbed as when she began.

Small wonder then that many mothers and fathers resist

going to a mental health professional for as long as possible—
or never go.

Since this book is largely based on the principles of Families Anonymous, very much a self-help organization, it has
emphasized the self-help approach. After all, nonprofessional-
ism—let's help ourselves rather than go to the so-called experts
—is the hallmark of all such organizations. Actually, though
some FA members have a strong bias against professional intervention, many others have attempted psychotherapeutic help
for themselves and/or for their children, either individually or
in family therapy. In some cases this has worked out; many
times it has not.

There's no way of knowing ahead of time, of course,
whether psychotherapy in any of its current forms will be
effective in your particular situation. Much depends on the
competence of the therapist and the nature of the problem.
Best candidates for therapy: frightened children, children with
phobias; neurotic children who still do cooperate to some extent with their parents—and who are therefore likely to cooperate with the therapist; children who are so anxious about
what's happening to them that they really want to go into
treatment. Worst candidates: children whose diagnosis is
"character disorder"—who have a hard time governing their
impulses; whose judgment is faulty; who can't seem to tolerate
frustration; whose perception of time is poor; who don't show
obvious anxiety when they get into trouble; whose sense of
reality is awry.

When might a parent fruitfully seek a consultation with
an outside professional? Oscar Rabinowitz, Assistant Executive
Director of Westchester Jewish Community Services, New
York, points to the following signs:

·The child mopes about, withdraws, shows obvious signs
of despondency or unhappiness for more than a couple of
weeks or so.

·There's evidence of "food fadism"—the child hardly

eats and loses a significant amount of weight.

·The child shows tremendous body concern—wants a nose job, a breast operation to make the breasts larger or smaller, et cetera.

·There are signs of drug abuse or addiction.

·The child has run away.

·There's evidence of sexual promiscuity or violence on the child's part.

·The child, upon becoming an adolescent, shows these significant changes: prefers isolation; has sudden, sharp difficulties in concentrating; thinks illogically; refuses to bathe or otherwise carry on a normal regimen of hygiene. Such changes are *possible* indicators of schizophrenia.

·The child has significant learning problems—may clown around in class, dislike studying, be rude to teachers. Such behavior may result from an undiagnosed learning problem, which in turn leads to rebelliousness. A thorough workup given by a psychologist may be indicated to see if there are any visual, perceptual, or auditory problems.

Of course, whatever the child's problem, if it makes the parents anxious or troubled, at least a consultation with an expert in adolescent behavior can prove helpful. The children don't necessarily have to be present at this stage. The parents may simply want to allay their own anxieties or gain more awareness of what's entailed in adolescent development or pick up some pointers on rearing or evaluating these children who are the object of their concern. Some therapists welcome such a consultation, which may also determine whether the child is a potentially appropriate candidate for psychotherapeutic intervention on either a short- or long-term basis. Other therapists prefer to see the child right away, with or without the parents; they don't want to give the child the impression they're working for the parents.

Summing all this up, Judith Lang, Assistant Director at the Jewish Board of Family and Children's Services, observes,

"If the parent has a sense that something out of the normal is going on—something bizarre and they become frightened by it—there's nothing lost in getting a consultation. It's far more constructive than being upset for a long period. The troubling behavior may be normal adolescent behavior of an extreme variety that will settle down in time, or it may be a sign of some deeper pathological process. Only a well-trained clinician can differentiate."

Why Adolescents Are Tough Patients

Any psychotherapist worth his state certification will tell you that, as a group, adolescents are the hardest category of patients to treat. Adolescent patients are generally so intense. Their moods are so changeable. Their emotional states vary so drastically: one hour they can love somebody, the next express intense dislike for them. Angry adolescents who come to the attention of psychiatrists and others in the mental health field may be so hostile that nobody, not even the professional, can genuinely like them. They may come into the office sullen, angry, objecting vociferously to their presence there, and making it clear that they were forced to come. They may not want to talk at all. Depending on the nature and degree of their troubled state, they may be so furiously distrustful of adults they will refuse to become engaged at all in the therapeutic process, as they will show by acting bored or restless, watching a spot on the ceiling, jiggling their feet, and so forth.

Some come to therapists' offices stoned, sit there like lumps, and stare glassy-eyed during the session. (In the case of drug addicts, no psychotherapy as such can take place until the patient is no longer addicted. As Dr. Leonard Siegel says, "You can't talk about psychological problems when the young person is addicted to hypnotic substances." So detoxification may have to precede psychotherapy.)

Not surprisingly, many psychiatrists, psychologists, and social workers in private practice refuse to take on adolescent patients for psychotherapy. They may not particularly like teenagers, or may even actively dislike them. They don't want to be burdened with patients who are so erratic and so difficult to teach. To be effective with teenagers, the therapist must genuinely like and respect them without becoming their advocate against their parents, must have an enormous fund of patience, and must be content with what might amount to small successes over long periods of time—if there's any success at all.

Which is better, someone in private practice or a caseworker (therapist) on the staff of a family service agency, child guidance clinic, or the like? There are highly skilled practitioners in private practice and on staff, and there are duds in both categories. Private practitioners charge hourly (45-minute) fees that range from $25 to $100 or so, depending on how long the clinician has been in practice, how well known he or she is in the field, and perhaps on what the traffic will bear. Psychiatrists charge the most; they are M.D.s and can prescribe medication when necessary, but in terms of skill in therapy they aren't necessarily any better than a well-trained clinical social worker.

You can look over the private practitioner, as it were, and go to someone else if you find there's no rapport; in an agency setting a caseworker is assigned to you or to your child, and in most instances a request to switch to another one isn't apt to be viewed too favorably. Agencies charge much lower fees than do most private practitioners; usually fees are set on a sliding scale and depend on the family's income and financial obligations. Another difference is that therapists in private practice are usually completely on their own, while caseworkers in agencies regularly report to supervisors who, in one way or another, check their work.

If you're seeking a therapist for yourself and/or your child, these are the most important characteristics to look for:

•Someone who has had solid experience working with adolescents.

•Someone who genuinely likes adolescents and seems sensitive to their needs and problems.

•Someone who doesn't make you feel it's all your fault.

•Someone whose basic conviction it is that, apart from other considerations, the young person in question *is* responsible for his or her actions.

•Someone *you* instinctively feel you can trust.

•Someone you find it easy to talk to.

•Someone you feel your teenager may like, trust, and talk to.

If you're considering therapy for your child, which is apt to be more fruitful—individual therapy or family therapy in which you, the parents, are also involved? Family therapy is very much "in" these days; the rationale is that the whole family has to be treated, or else the youth is returning to the same environment that helped precipitate the problem in the first place. But some experts in adolescent dynamics don't agree; they say that since adolescence is the time for separation from parents, the adolescent patients will be even more resistant to treatment if their parents are present. Sometimes it's suggested that parents be seen separately. But even if your child is in treatment alone, the principle that has received so much emphasis in this book—the importance of changing yourself—still applies.

You may have found the greatest therapist or clinic within a thousand miles; you still must get your child to agree to go. Don't be surprised if you don't get instant cooperation; as has been said, this depends on the nature and degree of the child's problems and his or her own view of them. *You* may think your child has problems; he or she may think you're the one who has them. Denial isn't the prerogative of any particular age group.

Understand that other things, too, are going on with your

child. Visiting a shrink is apt to make a child feel stigmatized, set apart. Even if all of you are in treatment—say, in family therapy—your rebellious child will still feel more like the patient because otherwise none of you would be there. Also, this child is likely to be singled out for special treatment—for instance, psychological testing.

And there are still more reasons for adolescent resistance. Just when it's important to show independence, the child is being asked to put himself or herself in the hands of another authority figure—that is, in another dependent position—and, worse, to express feelings, which he or she probably has a lot of trouble doing. Most importantly, the therapist very likely will be identified with the parents, either because they chose this therapist or because this person is an adult who shares the parents' power, or both, with the result that the child doesn't trust the therapist at all.

This lack of trust is the crux of why psychotherapy so often fails to reach adolescents. For psychotherapy to be effective, there has to be a bond of trust between the patient and the practitioner. The adolescent has to feel free enough to open up to the therapist, to love the therapist, to hate the therapist—to see the therapist at various times as mother, father, sibling, or teacher, or whoever else happens to be a disturbing influence. When adolescents first come into therapists' offices they're often so distrustful and so resistant that it may take even a very skillful therapist months to break down this resistance and establish the beginnings of a trusting relationship.

Sometimes it never happens. A number of FA families tell of their children being in treatment for several months, only to be suddenly told, "There's nothing I can do for your child." Assuming the therapist is a good and sympathetic one, those months aren't necessarily wasted. At least, on some level, the child may realize that the parents cared enough to consult a therapist, and this exposure may make treatment more acceptable at a later date. Whether this occurs also depends to some extent on the way the idea of going to a therapist was first presented to the child.

There are destructive and constructive approaches. One destructive way is to say, "You're impossible these days, and the therapist is going to change you so you'll be more the way we want you to be." Another destructive approach: "You've got all these terrible problems; the shrink will fix you up." Don't harp on the problems. Instead, convey that maybe there's something going on underneath, something that's making the child anxious and troubled. Make it clear that you, too, are anxious and troubled by what's going on, and—equally important—that going to a therapist for emotional problems is no different from going to a physician for physical problems.

You may get a flat turndown regardless of how you put it. Even if the child is also worried, he or she may not be able to admit it—especially to you. Besides, the need to rebel practically guarantees a negative reaction. What then? You can accept the decision gracefully, in hopes that maybe you'll have more success in a month or two or three. In fact, if you present the offer of therapy in a positive, noncoercive way, your child may find it easier to accept the idea a bit later.

What about coercion? What about trying to force your child to go into treatment? Clearly, this is antithetical to the principles put forward in this book (except possibly when the child is a clear danger to self or others). There are some professionals, however, who believe in the efficacy of coercion if a request doesn't work. One way to coerce is to give an ultimatum: "Either you go into therapy or you can no longer live at home." Another form of coercion would be to go into court, have the child declared incorrigible, and arrange for his or her placement in a residential treatment center or group home where therapy is also given.

This is the approach Robin and Theresa decided upon after they realized they had virtually no control over their fourteen-year-old son. He'd been stealing, selling marijuana, truant much of the time, and coming home at all hours of the night. They consulted someone at a child guidance clinic. After some investigation, the therapist advised them to go to Family Court, and upon consultation between parents, judge, and therapist, the boy was sent to a residential treatment center run by the clinic.

Whether or not such methods work may depend on how the parents present the issue to the child—whether they seem to be acting out of a genuine conviction that this is the only way left to help the child, or whether this is a way of punishing or getting rid of the child. Much also depends on the effectiveness of the therapist, agency, or treatment center to which the child is sent. There certainly are instances in which court-referred adolescents do finally accept treatment and begin to cope more constructively with their problems. This often happens in residential treatment centers where a great deal of warmth is shown and the child becomes part of the "family."

Unfortunately, there's a great scarcity of effective residential treatment centers, and many are quite expensive (though some state or local financial help is often available to parents).

Some rebellious young people are more inclined to go completely on their own to walk-in treatment centers especially set up for adolescents who reject traditional medical and mental health facilities. A few major cities have such centers, and some of the runaway houses around the country also welcome troubled youths, seeing them for counseling even if they aren't strictly runaways. There's a tremendous need for an expansion of such facilities. Unfortunately—again—they're scarce, and cutbacks in government funding have made them scarcer. But you might investigate to see if there is one in your area and, if so, suggest this approach to your child as an alternative. Your local family service or mental health agency should know if any are to be found locally.

17. How Families Anonymous Helps Parents

"My name is Sal," the tall, thin, bespectacled man sitting at one end of the long table said. He smiled as if to greet personally the other persons, sixteen in all, also seated around the table. Then he went on in his quiet yet emphatic way. "I'd like to tell you how it was before I joined Families Anonymous and what I've gotten out of FA. Our boy, our only child, started acting strangely when he turned eleven. He'd been doing pretty well in school, then he started underachieving, then he wouldn't go to school at all. Just flatly refused to go. Other things happened. He'd stay out later and later. There were things missing around the house.

"We thought, at the time, that our child was the only child doing that kind of thing. We felt so alone, so isolated. He was getting bigger and heavier—at twelve he had shot up to five-ten and weighed in at a hundred and sixty pounds—and we were getting to be smaller and thinner. We had some bitter fights and he threatened his mother and aunt.

"We couldn't handle him any more, and he became a ward of the court at thirteen. He messed up in one foster home and was sent to another. He ran away from that home, then somehow hooked up with an older girl. She was twenty-two, she had her own car, she took off with him to New York. The girl's mother called every day—she was convinced their bodies would turn up in the gutter, her daughter would be raped, and so on.

"Nothing happened. They came back from their joyride intact, but that couldn't be said for the rest of us. We wanted to help our child, but it seemed like everything we did was wrong. The boy would act—we'd react. And how we reacted! At one point my wife and I nearly broke up. Anyway, when he returned he was locked up; he'd violated his parole. Finally the judge remanded him to us—he said juvenile hall and foster homes weren't doing him any good.

"That's about when we joined FA—and, as I said, we were wrecks. What got us first, as far as FA is concerned, is that we weren't isolated any more. Here were loads of other people with stories like ours—worse, some of them. Yet these people had survived—they could even laugh about the horrors now; and it seemed like we hadn't laughed in years. We used to wring our hands wondering just where and how things had gone wrong. The old-timers said, 'We don't spend so much time on the past, on analysis. We concentrate on the here-and-now. On what we can do now to make our lives better.' We'd talked and talked and talked ourselves hoarse trying to reach our son. In FA they said, 'We don't bother doing that any more—we just shut up.'

"Boy, I didn't know how hard it is to shut up. But we did it finally, we got off his back—and that made our backs lighter, too. They talked a lot at FA meetings about not being doormats—and not allowing our buttons to be pushed. It took me a while to realize how my son used to set me up to make me feel guilty. Now I understand that what he does is his responsibility—now I don't have to feel guilty about what he does.

"He says he notices a change in his parents—we certainly don't have the bitter quarrels we used to have—but he still takes off now and then. He still won't go to school. When he leaves I think he goes to New York, hitchhikes there, but I can't be sure because if I ask him he clams up. He has two or three sets of ID's saying he's eighteen. A little while ago he was busted on a pot charge and asked us for money, but—thanks to FA—I've learned my lesson. I said no. He said he'd never see us again if we didn't give it to him, and my reply was that that's the way it would have to be.

"We learn to measure life in terms of small victories. He's fifteen now, still in the drug scene, but he doesn't threaten to beat up his mother any more. He doesn't take his mother's purse. We feel he's doing much better. He talks to us a little more than he did. We love him; his home is there when he wants it. He knows that. If he gets into trouble, though, he'll have to take responsibility for it. He knows that, too. What we've learned most of all is to take life one day at a time. We try not to look back. We try not to look ahead—to anticipate what other trouble our son might get into, what his future will be like. It's one day at a time."

WHAT FA OFFERS

Sal is a member of an FA group located in the Chicago area. The group meets once a week and Sal says he and his wife make every effort to attend the regular weekly meetings. Though he knows the program inside out by now, he feels that regular attendance helps him keep the principles—the principles he claims have been so helpful to him—firmly in mind. "It's so easy to slip back," he explains, "to try to change your child instead of yourself, to lecture and rescue, to condemn and criticize . . . You can't change the habits of a lifetime overnight, or even in three years, without some reinforcements. Going to meetings gives me that reinforcement."

Started by a group of parents of drug-addicted sons and daughters in the Los Angeles area in 1971, FA has grown spectacularly; by mid-1978 there were 115 groups in over 100 cities across the United States. Like Alcoholics Anonymous and Al-Anon, upon which it's patterned, FA has Twelve Steps which members follow as they "work" the program. (The Steps reflect such principles as the parents' admission of powerlessness and the taking of a personal inventory.) Like AA's and Al-Anon's, the Twelve Steps have strongly religious underpinnings, but atheists and agnostics as well as the devout belong to FA groups, and references to God in the Steps can be interpreted as liberally or as narrowly as one prefers. As an FA pamphlet states, thousands of nonbelievers "have been able to gain benefit from the Twelve Steps by using their own unique interpretation of a 'Power greater than ourselves.' "

FA members who commit themselves to the program benefit in a number of ways. Here are the main values they gain:

• The sympathy and support of a group of parents who are going through—or have gone through—similar experiences. The father of a girl who keeps threatening to commit suicide puts it like this: "Just being there, communing with people in your own position—that has been a great source of strength. We get an awful lot out of these other human beings—persons with names and faces and character and heart and soul who are suffering and concerned."

• The sharing of experiences. While it's against FA principles to give others direct advice, members try to be as helpful as they can in revealing what has worked for *them*.

• "Role models" of sorts—other members who have gone through the same ordeals and are now in a much better place in life—including numerous members who can speak of problem children who have gotten better.

• The constant reminder that they can't change their children—that the children are responsible for their actions good and bad.

• Outside support in times of crisis or when things just

seem unbearable. Members in most groups exchange phone numbers, and many freely call each other for help and sharing between meetings.

•Encouragement to change themselves—to grow.

•A deepening understanding of the fact that when a young person is in trouble his family, too, is in trouble—and also needs and deserves help.

•Encouragement to release with love—to gain some emotional distance from the turmoil created by the rebellious child. As one member says, "What impressed me most when I first joined FA was the thoroughness with which some members had detached themselves from really horrendous situations. They'd gotten to the point where they were able to be concerned without becoming so emotionally involved."

At the core of FA (and all other self-help groups) is a fundamental conviction: Only those who have suffered through the problem know what it feels like—and it's they who can be most helpful to others going through the same ordeal.

FA meetings follow a specific format—the same one whether the gathering takes place in Torrance, California, Lexington, Kentucky, or Chicago, Illinois. A different FA member leads the meeting each week, to emphasize the fact that there is no single leader and to give everyone a chance to be involved. Meetings generally begin with a reading of the Serenity Prayer made so popular by AA, then follow a prescribed format that includes group discussion of a particular topic and a question-and-answer period for newcomers. Members remain determinedly anonymous at meetings and on a public level, referring to each other only by their first names in group discussions. Like most self-help groups, FA also remains steadfastly nonprofessional; almost without exception no mental health professionals participate in their capacity as professionals. Often one member, usually a longtime veteran, talks at length about the way the program has helped him or her, just as Sal did at that Chicago meeting.

WHY THEY LEAVE—AND STAY

Some people attend two or three meetings and are hooked on FA; some go once or twice and drop out. They drop out because the group obviously doesn't meet their expectations. It doesn't meet the expectations of parents who, in effect, want child-rearing instruction; such instruction is, after all, incompatible with the aims and philosophy of the organization. Many of the people who leave do so before they really get the point of the repeated statement that you're powerless over your children's behavior; they simply interpret this to mean the ultimate in permissiveness, letting the children do anything they want. Some drop out because they're not hurting enough as yet, or feel uncomfortable in group situations, or resent needing the help of a self-help group—or because that particular group isn't well run.

As with the "powerless" concept, more than a few mothers and father who initially attend FA meetings are shocked to hear the release-with-love principle espoused, especially from parents who chose to release their children in the ultimate way —forbidding them to live at home any more, maybe even changing the door locks on them.

"I was a trembling, shaking mess," recalls the mother of a boy who has been arrested for stealing, trespassing, and disturbing the peace. "I was talking and crying uncontrollably. But after that first night I started listening. Some of the things that you hear in the beginning sound absolutely heartless and mean—how can anyone throw away their child? But gradually I learned to have an open mind."

Finally, when her own boy turned seventeen and had had four car accidents in six weeks (driving illegally and without insurance) and yet another police arrest, she asked him to go live with his father, who resided in another state. He refused. So she simply told him to leave. He did. Now, she says, he has his own apartment and is improving.

She'd felt so alone, this woman says, so different—that meeting other parents in similar or worse situations was a revelation to her. There were in her group a dentist, a business-man and his wife, a couple consisting of an attorney husband and a wife who was a legal secretary, a truckdriver and his waitress wife—"all of them respectable, responsible people. Somehow that made me feel much better." She gained some perspective: Listening to stories more awful than her own, she could honestly come away feeling, "Heavenly days, my child isn't the worst one in the world, after all!" She got a great deal out of listening to other parents relate their experiences. " 'Did my son feel that way?' I'd wonder, hearing another mother talk about her troubled son. Or, listening to some parents talk about the things they wanted to change in themselves, I'd ask myself, 'Did I behave the way that parent says he did?' And sometimes I'd have to say, 'That's right, that's just the way I acted.' Then I knew I had to do something about myself."

STARTING A NEW GROUP

FA members meet in rooms donated by churches, banks, schools, hospitals, and similar public places. Meetings are free, but each week the hat is passed for donations to defray the cost of refreshment, literature, and other expenses, including a small contribution to the organization donating the space. New groups are started periodically in towns and cities where there are none—usually by a troubled parent who has somehow read or heard something about FA.

So it was in Martha's case. Martha's son had turned from an "angel" to a pothead and runaway after he and his family moved from the middle west to a major eastern city, on the heels of which event his father was revealed as an alcoholic. Upon reading about FA in *Good Housekeeping* magazine, Martha sent away for a packet of literature from FA's World

Service Headquarters in Torrance, California. (The address appears on the following page.) Martha also asked FA headquarters how she could find other people in her area interested in joining a group. FA had on file the names of other parents whose boys or girls were committing disturbing acts and sent these names to her. Starting out with several interested parties, she held meetings in her home. Soon, however, she suggested that all those then attending—six people—approach various churches and synagogues in the area to see if one of them would donate meeting space one day a week. Such space was quickly found and, at last report, the group was growing.

"What's happened to me," says Martha now, "is that after I was in the program for a while I stopped feeling so ashamed of my child, so ashamed of my role as a parent. As long as I read myself as a failure, it made my child a failure, too. But as this awful guilt I felt started to leave—that took some time, it wasn't easy—I could have better feelings about myself and about the worth of my child, too. If I'm no longer a failure it means I'm at least something of a success—and if I am, so's my child."

Martha paused to reflect a moment, then added, "Throughout these hurting times I was going through—and to some extent still am—the Serenity Prayer has helped a lot to sustain me, too. 'God grant me the serenity to accept the things I cannot change; the courage to change the things I can; and the wisdom to know the difference.' That's been so comforting. Parents who go through what we go through need to be comforted."

Readers who wish to obtain information about the Families Anonymous group in their area or to start a new group may contact Families Anonymous, Inc., P.O. Box 344, Torrance, CA 90501. To help defray costs (including postage), FA charges $1.00 for a packet of informational materials.